Stand Out Social Marketing

6 Keys to Rise Above the Noise,
Differentiate Your Brand,
and Build an Outstanding
Online Presence

Mike Lewis

@bostonmike

New York   Chicago   San Francisco   Lisbon   London
Madrid   Mexico City   Milan   New Delhi
San Juan   Seoul   Singapore   Sydney   Toronto

The **McGraw·Hill** Companies

1 2 3 4 5 6 7 8 9 0   DOC/DOC   1 8 7 6 5 4 3 2

ISBN   978-0-07-179496-1
MHID   0-07-179496-4

e-ISBN 978-0-07-179497-8
e-MHID   0-07-179497-2

McGraw-Hill books are available at special quantity discounts to use as premiums and sales promotions or for use in corporate training programs. To contact a representative, please e-mail us at bulksales@mcgraw-hill.com.

This book is printed on acid-free paper.

In loving memory of Uncle Frank and Aunt Mary
I wish you were both here to celebrate
this accomplishment with me.

To the love of my life and my best friend, Sheila
Thanks for your unending and overwhelming
love and support ,without which I would never
have been able to complete this book.

To my little buddy, Frankie, and my baby doll, Vienna.
You will always be my greatest achievements.

CONTENTS

Part 3: Summarizing Stand Out

Foreword

With so many companies diving into social marketing, separating the noise from the chaff will be a challenge; as a result, differentiation on social channels is critical for brand success. Savvy marketers know that they must create a new playbook beyond traditional tactics, starting with a deeper look at the core brand presence. In fact, your approach will have to take root in how you manage the internal operations of your social media strategy. Your approach to social media and the behind-the-scenes strategy is the key to differentiation and your brand's success on the social web.

Most outsiders quickly dismiss successful social media programs as being easy—but like an iceberg, what people perceive online is just the tip of it: the true weight of the effort stems from a company getting prepared the right roles, policies, processes, and more. At the time this book was written most companies have yet to reach social business maturity—the average corporate social business program is only three years old—yet some companies are already defining best practices. But what's generating all the noise? More specifically, what are the obstacles to turning out a mature and focused social media strategy?

A recent report published by my firm, the Altimeter Group, titled "A strategy for Managing Social Media Proliferation," uncovered some of the challenges that make social media so difficult for brands to differentiate and manage. First, consider that, on average, 70 percent of enterprises said that social media efforts meet business objectives. Yet an average of just 43 percent said they had a formalized strategy roadmap that addresses how social media will meet specific business goals. With a lack of clear strategy and objectives the ability to differentiate your presence becomes far more difficult.

Second, Altimeter found that on average companies have a whopping 178 discrete social media accounts in their global corporation, not including employee accounts. Further, most companies do not even have accurate inventory of their existing assets. The deluge of accounts and confusion will only be exacerbated as more business units adopt social media—especially within distributed organizations. This gigantic management obstacle makes it impossible for social media strategists to gain a holistic view of the corporate strategy, again hindering the ability to differentiate your social presence.

Stand Out Social Marketing succeeds in focusing on the strategies and tactics to help brands differentiate and rise above the noise on the social web. Mike's unique ability is in presenting complex topics within an easily digestible framework, enabling marketers to implement these strategies in their company. As a seasoned social marketer, Mike also provides detailed case studies that will help marketers understand how top brands, along with some unknown but creative companies, are implementing these strategies in their business.

Most uniquely, the book provides actionable recommendations made for each user, individually based, on a maturity score assigned at the outset. It allows less-savvy users to truly understand how they can improve and learn from those who achieve a higher maturity score. In this way, Mike's book is an important tool for each and every one of us.

With so many jumping onto social media, it is the right time for this book: you *must* stand out. As Mike correctly points out, competition on social media is not only with your direct competitors, but with every other brand vying for the attention of the audience. Applying a Stand Out approach will help differentiate your brand and set you apart from the pack.

Jeremiah Owyang
Industry Analyst, Partner
Altimeter Group

Acknowledgments

Near the start of this project my wife and I welcomed our beautiful daughter, Vienna Marie Lewis, to our family. There have only been a few times in my life when I have deeply underestimated the impact of a single event and this was one of them. I am proud to say, however, while I grossly underestimated the amount of time I would be able to dedicate to writing P.V. (i.e., post-Vienna's arrival), I also deeply underestimated the amount of love I would have for her.

Reflecting on the experience of writing this book I recall the words of my economics professor from grad school who once reminded me *that which doesn't kill you will only make you stronger.* When I took on this challenge I didn't realize that I would be faced with multiple life events (highlighted by the birth of Vienna)

that would both impact the writing of this and motivate me to push the bounds of what I believed I was capable of and force me well beyond my comfort zone. That said, I would not have been able to complete this book without the help and support of some very important people.

For those that know me well it will come as no surprise that there are thousands of individuals I would like to thank for helping me make this book possible. I feel both fortunate and privileged to be surrounded by so many individuals who continue to guide, encourage, and teach me while showering me with support, especially during times when completing this book seemed overwhelming and impossible.

MY STAND OUT FAMILY

To my best friend and love of my life, Sheila. You constantly encouraged me through the intense, crazy days of this process. You gave me the freedom to write on my schedule and stood behind me when I doubted myself. Without your sacrifices, this book would never have been written. I will never forget that support and I love you more and more each day.

Thanks to Vienna and Frankie. You are both too young to realize it but your smiling faces, hugs, and kisses during this process gave me the strength to complete this book. I said it before and I'll say it again, you both will always be my greatest achievements.

Thanks Mom! For being the strongest woman I will ever know, my biggest fan and constant advocate. You taught me how to write and continue to challenge me to fulfill my dreams.

Thanks Dad, you inspired me to get into "computers" at a very young age and supported my passions throughout my life. You taught me to question, think, and chase my dreams.

To my little sister, Mim (my second-biggest fan). Thanks for always being there and supporting me. You are not only my sister but also one of my best friends, and I am very proud of you.

To my "brother from another mother," Randy. Thanks for always been a source of unending strength and encouragement in good times and bad. You helped give me the downtime I needed to relax and enjoy life during the most stressful times of this process.

To my other mom and dad, Nancy and Phil, you both have always believed in me and been a consistent support system for me, especially during particularly difficult times in my life.

I am extremely fortunate to be surrounded by an intimate family who have showered me with support and encouragement throughout my life and continue to inspire me throughout this process. Thanks to Victor and Alex for showing me that even in the toughest times it's possible to smile; to Paulette for everything you do to help our family and for your unending love; to Bobbie for being a continuous support system for Sheila and me; Ricky for being a friend, brother, and confidant; Alison for being a great cousin and friend; Nora for your love and support, Auntie Bernie and Uncle Gary for always being my other set of parents and for your continuous support; and last but certainly not least my brother-in-law, "Mad Dog" Dan Madden, on the most stressful nights you were always just what the doctor ordered. Thank you all. You mean more to me than words can say.

Finally, huge thanks, and a toast, to my wolf pack. "You guys might not know this, but I consider myself a bit of a loner. I tend to think of myself as a one-man wolf pack. But when I first met Randy at age one, I knew he was one of my own. And my wolf pack...it grew by one. So there... there were two of us in the wolf pack... I was alone first in the pack, and then Randy joined in later. And when Mim brought Dan home, I thought, 'Wait a second, could it be?' And now I know for sure, I just added another guy to my wolf pack. Three of us wolves running around the streets of Burlington, betting on football, fishing, lighting off fireworks, and doing sake bombs. So tonight, I make a toast!"

(Taken from *The Hangover*... slightly modified...)

MY STAND OUT FRIENDS

My closest friends helped keep me sane during this process. Whether it was taking me out for a much-needed drink, giving me a call to see how things were going, or stopping by to light a fire and watch the Sox on the big screen in my backyard, they helped to relieve the stress and kept me focused on making this book happen. To my closest friends and support system, thank you. Steve Tremblay, you never let me stop believing and got me out to chill for lunch or for a drink after work. My wing man, Brett Bell, with whom I have shared Red Sox season tickets since we graduated from Bentley. Todd Hughey, who shares my passion for music and Boston sports. To Jonathan Tang, who started as a mentor and grew into a close friend. Karen Sheehey, who I shared an office with for over five years and who grew to become one of my closest friends. Christine Major, who has been a colleague and inspired me to test my hand at stand-up comedy. Julie Devoll, who has been a close friend since the Stonehill days, and Christie Corchran, who will always be my West Coast girlfriend. Chrissy and S for your constant support and encouragement. The Bradford Guys (Bri, Jer, Biscuit, Stinch, Q-Dog, Skinny, and Bull). Nat Rink and my hoops team (Cassel, Jay, Jedi, Vidit, Ribs, Moon, and Dan) for putting up with me missing so many games throughout the process. Thanks!

THE STAND OUT TEAM AT AWARENESS

I could not have accomplished this without the help of the outstanding team at Awareness. Most especially, our executive team, Brian Zanghi, Dave Carter, Steve Tremblay, and Melissa Leffler, who continue to support, encourage, and inspire me on a daily basis.

To the entire Awareness Family especially Sal Giliberto, Jeff Gaffny, Liane Harrington, Erin Hegarty, Molly Cunningham,

Joe Payne, Keith Sullivan, Matt Kusch, Melissa DiPietro, Steve Owen, Ken Cyr, Heidi Wong, Jesse Richard, Lisa Connor, Damian Plummer, Issaam Gharios, Michael Wineburg, Todd Kirkland, Nikhil Lakshminarayanan, Dawei Wang, Christine Albert, Brent Dubecki, Pete Oliver, Mark Wylie, Ryan Triggs, and Aaron Fleming.

Also, a big thanks to our stand out board of directors, Carol Meyers, Dayna Grayson, Rich D'Amore, and Ron Nordin, for being a great support to the business and our mission.

To some Stand Out people who have moved on from Awareness but remain friends in my life including John Bruce, Mark Cattini, Robin Hopper, Steve Richards, Will "I Am" Eisner, Scott "Chewie" Farrell, Ashley Quincey, Naomi Marr, and Robin "R2" Dindayal.

TO OUR STAND OUT CUSTOMERS AND PARTNERS

Our customers (some of which are featured in this book) continue to be a stream of support and inspiration. I especially want to thank Rick Racela of Comcast SportsNet, David Balcome and Karen Rose of American Cancer Society, Holly Spring of Nuance, Andrew Patterson and Alicia Mullen of Major League Baseball, Jonas Nielson of Mindjumpers, Justin Holmerud of Starwood, Katie Stanke of Zynga, James Hart of ASOS, Russ Debenport of Compassion International, Taulbee Jackson of Raidious, Dominic Mills of Auros, Dave Kerpen of Likeable, Bryan Gonzalez of Fox, Christine Major of DemandWare, Marcy Cohen of Sony Electronics, Steve Gadecki of Sony Pictures TV, Jim Carey from WannaBee Social, Mark Parker of Smart Social Media, Julie Devoll of *Harvard*

Business Review and the hundreds of clients and partners I know I am forgetting.

STAND OUT WORK INSPIRATIONS

Throughout my career I have had the honor of working with several leaders who have grown to become mentors and friends. In their own way each of these individuals has had a part in shaping my career and served as the inspiration for many of the stories contained in this book. A special thanks to George Bloom, Dave Thurman, John Foley, Chris Brogan, Aaron Kahlow, John Brodeur, C.C. Chapman, Joe Pulizzi, Rich Perkett, David Meerman Scott, Jason Falls, Cappy Popp, Jason Keath, Yonald Cherry, Bruce Weinberg, and John Sisson.

STAND OUT GUIDANCE AND SUPPORT

A HUGE thank-you to a Stand Out group of individuals who provided detailed guidance throughout the writing and editing process. This group of people offered outstanding support by helping to review my work, offering their suggestions, and challenging me to improve. A very special thanks to:

- Brian Zanghi, who is helping guide my career path and has grown to become a mentor and friend.
- Dave Carter, who has shared both the vision and passion to build a *Stand Out* company.

- Dave Kerpen, a very "likeable" friend who helped teach me the "ins and outs" of becoming an author while helping me navigate the system.
- Jon Wortman, a coach and mentor who continuously provided feedback and criticism while helping me to "master communication at work."
- Jeremiah Owyang, a friend and colleague who provided feedback and direction throughout the entire process.
- Lora Kratchonouva, a friend and master networker who helped me focus my thoughts and encouraged me to get my ideas on paper.
- Erik Qualman, an inspiring individual and friend who continually asked me "when is your book coming out?" and helped to motivate me to write.
- Steve Tremblay, who is the most technology and marketing savvy finance guy I know. Thanks for being a friend and for your constant support throughout the process.
- Last but not least, Paul Gillin. Paul has grown to become a friend and trusted advisor. I read his book, *The New Influencers* when it was first released and I was lucky enough to have the chance to work with him directly as we planned and launched the first New Marketing Summit some years after. His guidance has helped me throughout my career and I look forward to returning the favor for him in the near future.

A STAND OUT TEAM

This book would never have got off the ground if not for the assistance and help from three Stand Out contributors. Jenn Reilly of

Scratch Marketing for helping to format all the charts, images, and pictures in this book. Liz Warburton, who was more than an editor, she was a fresh set of eyes and the constant cure for writer's block. Her collaborative guidance throughout the process was the catalyst to help get this book completed. Sal Giliberto is my right-hand man at Awareness and true expert in the social media and marketing space. His insights and collaboration not only helped with the development of the concept of this book but also drove the content and flow. I am looking forward to helping him launch and publish his first book.

THE STAND OUT PUBLISHING FAMILY AT MCGRAW-HILL

A heartfelt thank-you to the editors and staff at McGraw-Hill. You inspired, challenged, and continuously pushed me to take the content to the next level. A very special thank-you to Stephanie Frerich, who inherited this project but quickly made it her own. Thanks for your support, encouragement, and honest feedback.

Finally, I want to sincerely thank everyone who didn't believe I could pull this off. My motivation to prove you wrong was a huge motivator throughout this process.

Introduction

The company would not survive if we couldn't stand out from the pack.

Founded by entrepreneurs Jonathan Tang and Rich Perkett in 1999, Salesnet was one of the early innovators in the OnDemand CRM (customer relationship management) software market. By 2006 the space was highly competitive and Salesforce.com had become the 800-pound gorilla and was growing like a weed. The market was moving at warp speed, and establishing a distinctive brand was the only option Salesnet had to compete.

I accepted the final changes on the very first blog post I had ever published, and it went live with little fanfare; recognition came only from the few that understood how different it was. In the eyes of the company the blog was simply a test of whether or not we could generate results by publishing our own content and ideas to a platform that we controlled. To me, it was much bigger: it was our opportunity to set ourselves apart and stand out from the crowd.

Up until that blog went live the company could best be classified as *competitively similar*. All the players in the CRM space offered similar messaging, which confused the audience and made differentiation impossible. In that environment, it seemed that the deepest pockets were the ones to succeed and the rest were devoured by the market's general sameness.

As I expected, and as the company discovered, our blog set Salesnet apart immediately. Employees and guest bloggers posted SEO-friendly topics and hot-button issues daily. The blog steadily grew in popularity with more and more people subscribing, commenting, forwarding, and engaging with the content. That engagement led to sales conversions, and the "blog leads" were two times more likely to close versus leads developed through traditional channels. It became the focal point of our marketing and sales initiatives and inspired the resurgence of a brand that moved from being *competitively similar* to *stand out*.

Brands competing on the social web face a similar, daunting challenge—with so many platforms and so many companies engaging in the social web, how can you stand out? The answer: differentiate or get lost in a web of sameness.

A STAND OUT SHOCK JOCK

How can such a polarizing figure generate so much success? Love him or hate him, Howard Stern is one of the most well known, successful, and distinctive radio personalities of all time. The self-proclaimed "King of All Media" is not only the king of the radio airways; he has released two *New York Times* bestsellers, a major motion picture, runs two channels on SiriusXM Satellite Radio, has his own cable On Demand TV channel, and is a judge on *America's Got Talent*.

His success was built on his distinctness. Throughout his long career Howard has been able to differentiate himself unlike any other radio personality. The "why" and "how" of this can be directly applied to how companies should approach social media if they want to stand out.

This book explores six areas of social media that businesses can use to differentiate and stand out from the pack. They include Presence, Paying Attention, Interaction, Content, Management, and Measurement.

When you apply these principles of differentiation to the *Stern Show*, it's easy to understand how Howard was able to amass so much success over the years.

- **A royal presence:** Howard's differentiated presence and his personality allowed him to consistently win over local markets by creating something more distinctive than the scripted programs of the other DJs he competed against.

- **Always paying attention and interacting:** The show is one of the first to move beyond a focus on conversations with guests. It's different in that the conversations have centered around listeners, and the show is based on where these groups take the conversation.

- **The king of all content:** The *Stern Show* revolves around new and unique content; interviews with guests are only a portion of the content served up daily.

- **Managing and organizing:** Howard and his team are laser focused each day on the general management of the show, from scheduling and inviting guests, to the interview formats and briefing, to games and bits. Everything is managed in a detailed format to ensure on-air success.

- **Measurement:** Measurement on the *Stern Show* has always focused on one key indicator—the ratings—which drive advertising revenue. Since his move to SiriusXM, the new focus is on subscribers.

When you roll it all together, Howard's stand out approach to his show is exactly how brands need to approach social media: establish presence, pay attention to your audience, generate meaningful content, and set up relevant systems to manage and measure your impact. The formula is the same for everyone, but the makeup of each piece is distinctively based on your own company, brand, and mission.

You have something unique to offer the marketplace; it's why you went into business in the first place. There's no reason to throw your hands up in the air in the face of a new online environment and resort to the same tactics and messaging as everyone else in the market. Build a distinctive position, differentiate your approach, and you will be able to set yourself apart.

BEING THE SAME IS THE RISKIEST THING YOU CAN DO

How many brands do you follow on Facebook and Twitter? How many of them truly differentiate themselves from the pack?

Social media is forcing a marketing renaissance and is ushering in an era of complexity, forcing brands to adapt. On the social web brands don't just compete with their direct competitors, they compete with *all* other brands in a constant war for the attention of the billions who occupy social networks. In this environment standing out isn't just important, *it's do or die.*

The basic human behavior of imitation is defining the playing field in social media: the innovators are being followed, liked, and copied. Like a team of youth soccer players, brands tend to chase the ball around the field with little to no organization. As a result these brands end up developing similar concepts, strategies, and ideas with subtle differentiation, leaving the audience overwhelmed, confused, and tired.

Your audience is pleading with you to forge a distinctive path. Your fans crave innovation and distinctness. To be successful, brands need to move from increased similarity to standing out with real differentiation. In short, being the same in social media is the riskiest thing you can do.

WHY THIS BOOK WAS WRITTEN

My company, Awareness, Inc., powers the social marketing strategies for hundreds of companies, allowing them to convert social marketing activities into leads and customers. We provide software that enables companies to manage their overall social media presence, engage with their audience, and capture & track detailed sales information. As vice president of sales and marketing I am fortunate to work with a large and diverse group of brands that represent a cross section of social media maturity. Over the course of our engagements, one challenge has risen above all the others: differentiation. As a result, the strategy, vision, and technology that Awareness provides tackle the problem of differentiation head-on. My particular focus is on driving sales through a differentiated social media strategy, and I have watched the strategies and tactics presented in this book lead to success at even the smallest companies. Invigorated by the results we have seen and the experience I have gathered from years of navigating the social media landscape, I am extremely proud to present the process of social marketing differentiation to you throughout the next 250 pages. I hope you carry these strategies over to your business as you move forward toward increased success.

WHAT THIS BOOK IS

- **This book is for social media and marketing practitioners, business owners, CEOs, and marketing executives.** The primary audiences for this book are marketers who are engaged in executing marketing programs for your company. It's also for the business owners who are looking to get more out of social media.

- **What's next:** If you have set up your social presence, taken the advice of all the gurus, but are wondering "what's next?" to continue to improve your strategy, this book is for you. It will demonstrate how to get the most out of your social activities and optimize what you are currently doing.

- **Bottom-line results:** If you are wondering how the bottom-line results are tied to social media, this book is for you. It will highlight areas where you can get more from your marketing and how it will impact the bottom line of your business.

ORGANIZING STAND OUT SOCIAL MARKETING

Taking a holistic approach is necessary as you differentiate your brand on the social web. There are six areas we highlight in this book to make sure you have everything you need to be successful.

PART 1: UNDERSTANDING STAND OUT

Chapter 1: Stand Out sets the foundation of the book and further explains the premise while defining what brands need to be doing as they differentiate their social media strategy.

PART 2: STAND OUT IN PRACTICE

Chapter 2: Stand Out by Paying Attention introduces the concept of paying attention while providing a framework to develop the first steps to your company's social media strategy.

Chapter 3: Stand Out by Paying Attention to Behaviors expands on the concept paying attention by providing strategies and tactics to help you gather the key information that comes from paying attention well. This chapter will help to focus your strategy by zeroing in on the behaviors, conversations, and individuals that matter most to your business.

Chapter 4: Stand Out Interactions addresses the next big step: interacting with your customer base. This chapter dives into the "what, why, and how" of making your interactions on social media stand out.

Chapter 5: The Science of Stand Out Interactions digs deeper into interactions by presenting the science behind the best strategic interactions. Learn the best days, times, and frequencies to get the most interaction from each piece of content.

Chapter 6: Stand Out Approaches to Stimulating Interaction presents 11 ways you can increase interactions at your company.

Chapter 7: Stand Out Content investigates how you can create content that rises above the noise on the social web, while highlighting case studies of brands that stand out through the content they deliver on social media.

Chapter 8: Stand Out Presence features the ways you can create a distinctive presence across all the social channels you participate in.

Chapter 9: Stand Out Management guides you through the back-end processes of developing a distinctive strategy. This includes discussions on teams, workflows, and policies.

Chapter 10: Stand Out by Measuring for ROI provides a detailed look at how you can measure and gauge the success of your strategy. Part of standing out is making sure you measure the right things and keep an accurate eye on trends.

PART 3: SUMMARIZING STAND OUT

Chapter 11: Performing a Stand Out Social Marketing Audit provides a framework to audit your current strategy while offering next steps to build out and improve your program.

Chapter 12: Out Standing! summarizes the key themes of the book while offering an action plan for the future.

LET'S CONNECT!

Let's face it, writing a book is kind of an old-school thing. It's a great vehicle for me to share my ideas with you, but it doesn't allow me to easily get your feedback. *And trust me, I want your feedback!* I want to connect with you and understand what you are thinking. Having a better picture of the specific challenges *you* face and *your* business objectives I am better able to serve you through the information I provide. To that end there are a bunch of ways for you to reach out and connect with me directly. If you need clarification as you read through the book, if you want to ask questions, if you need advice, *anything*—please reach out using any of the mechanisms below.

E-mail: mike@standoutsocialmarketing.com

Website and Blog: http://www.standoutsocialmarketing.com

Twitter: @bostonmike

Facebook: http://facebook.com/bostonmike

LinkedIn: http://www.linkedin.com/in/lewismich

In addition, I want to make this book as interactive and engaging as possible. To that end there are words and phrases throughout the book that are highlighted LIKE THIS. (Huge shout-out to Adam Metz, author of *The Social Customer* for giving me this idea!) To get additional content, offers, and downloads that will extend your experience with the book, simply go to http://www.standoutsocialmarketing.com and enter the highlighted word or phrase in the search box. You will immediately be directed to the additional material.

On http://www.standoutsocialmarketing.com you will find a vast amount of resources that will extend the concepts presented in this book. Integrated into that site you will find:

- **Stand out strategies:** Case studies featuring brands with a differentiated approach to social media

- **Stand out strategists:** The individuals who have implemented Stand Out strategies within their business.

- **Stand out statistics:** A database of infographics featuring the latest and greatest details on the changing landscape of social media.

- **Stand out blog:** A collection of blog posts featuring some of the greatest thinkers in the social media space.

Finally, if you are inspired to tweet about the book as you read, I encourage you to use the hashtag #StandOut so we can all join in the conversation!

TAKE THE RED PILL!!

In the 1999 blockbuster *The Matrix*, Neo is asked to make a choice. Choose the red pill and gain greater insight into the world of the Matrix or take the blue pill and return to the normal, everyday life he already knows. Modern marketers are at a crossroads and face the same decision. Choose the red pill and stand out, or take the blue pill and continuing operating in a world of marketing sameness.

Those taking the red pill will find more opportunities as they are speaking to their audience in the manner that today's consumers prefer. These marketers choose to participate in the revolution and work to define standards, metrics, and the landscape of the social media universe. Those opting for the blue pill will be left to sit back as the world morphs without them.

From here on out I encourage you to take the red pill, dive into a new world, and remember to fasten your seat belt: the old world of marketing is going *bye-bye*!

CHAPTER 1

Stand Out

Stand out experiences have the power to change brand perception, drive customer loyalty, increase revenue, and build deep relationships.

When I travel, I do whatever I can to get home as early as possible. That means cobbling together flight itineraries that get me home quickly. Logging hundreds of thousands of miles split between several carriers isn't ideal, and if you traveled as frequently as I do, you would think that, at some point, I would have picked an airline and stuck with it. Today I have, but it wasn't until I was *wowed* by a stand out approach to customer service just a couple of years ago.

It was February 2010, and I was off to Tampa, Florida to speak at Jason Keath's Social Fresh Conference. On this particular occasion, I flew Delta Airlines and arrived at Tampa early the morning of February 8. I delivered the session, spent some time networking, and hurried back to the airport to catch the evening flight home.

On the way to the airport I checked my flight status and, lo and behold, I discovered that I was headed to the airport *on the wrong day.* My flight was scheduled to depart Tampa at the same time the following day. As you can imagine, I panicked and did what anyone would: I called Delta to sort this mess out. The Delta representative I spoke to told me he could help but that I would have to stay on the phone with him for about 30 minutes, due to a computer system issue. I thought nothing of it, and we made small talk as he maneuvered through the painstaking process of rebooking my flight.

After some small talk and banter—*Success!* I was booked on that night's flight and made it to the gate just as the doors of the plane were closing. The flight attendant had just jumped on the P.A. and told us to stow our electronic devices as I sent out a tweet:

> On @delta flight leaving Tampa . . . Can't wait to get home. Side note, @delta cust srv rocks . . . Said it before & continue to be impressed.

I arrived home a couple of hours later and was greeted at the front door by a very excited two-year-old boy who's always happy when Dad makes it home on time.

I thought nothing of the tweet I had sent, until the next morning, when I checked Twitter and found a response from @DeltaBlog:

Thanks for your comment. We hope you had a great trip home to that new baby!

"To that new baby," I thought. "How the heck did they know that?"

Let me explain *what I thought had happened* before I let you in on the reality. During that conversation with Delta Customer Service I thought they had strategically collected and recorded information on me in their customer relationship management (CRM) system. The data collected during our conversation allowed Delta to build out a broad and deep customer profile on me. I assumed that my tweet triggered an alert, letting Delta know I had made a comment. Someone on the social media team saw the comment, pulled up my profile, and replied with a personalized message that was based on the details in my profile. "Amazing," I thought.

It was such a stand out experience for me that I immediately contacted Delta to understand what happened behind the scenes. That's when Delta's Social Media Manager, Rachael Rensink, shed some light on *what actually happened*. She reminded me that the day I was traveling back to Boston was also the day of one of the worst blizzards to hit the Washington, D.C., area. It dumped several feet of snow in the region and caused significant travel delays across the country. Rachael, who was monitoring Twitter that day, was inundated with negative tweets from weary travelers and was doing her best to resolve as many issues as possible. My tweet represented the lone piece of positive sentiment in a sea of negativity. When she saw it, she clicked through to my profile, went to my blog, learned about my background, and concluded that I must be hurrying home to see my son. She had singled me out and responded accordingly.

Delta's approach was stand out. Rachael did not simply respond to my tweet with a canned response; she paid attention and went the extra mile to personalize the interaction. This was a rare "customer wow moment" and a stand out example of a brand "paying attention." For the first time in years of flying, I was able to connect with an airline carrier on a one-to-one basis, and in a way that didn't involve sitting on hold for 45 minutes until someone had time for me. This time they reached out to me in a direct, simple, meaningful, and personalized way. This immediately humanized the brand's image, made Delta more than a faceless company, and created real brand loyalty in a customer. Since this experience Delta has remained my carrier of choice.

Social media offers the opportunity to create unique experiences like this, which lead to lasting connections. This is why using social media to stand out is so important. It offers brands the ability to create relationships and create a lifetime of loyalty.

A STAND OUT CHALLENGE

Standing out is the biggest challenge marketers will face in 2013. At its core, standing out is about a brand's ability to forge a distinctive strategy in social media. For the purposes of providing background, *Wikipedia* defines differentiation as the following:

> In economics and marketing, product differentiation (also known simply as "differentiation") is the process of distinguishing a product or offering from others, to make it more attractive to a particular target market. This involves differentiating it from competitors' products as well as a firm's own product offerings. The concept was proposed by Edward Chamberlin in his 1933 Theory of Monopolistic Competition.
>
> For businesses, differentiation can be a source of competitive advantage. Marketing or product differentiation is the process of describing the differences between products or services, or the resulting list of differences. This is done in order to demonstrate the unique aspects of a firm's product and to create a sense of value. Marketing textbooks are firm on the point that any differentiation must be valued by buyers. The term "unique selling proposition" refers to advertising to communicate a product's differentiation.[1]

The objective of differentiation is to build a market position that potential customers see as unique. On social media, differences in

HOW DELTA STOOD OUT

- **Stand out by paying attention:** Delta didn't just listen to what I was saying; they paid attention to my situation holistically. It would have been just as easy to say "Thanks for the tweet!" Instead, they went the extra mile to personalize the interaction.

- **Stand out interactions:** They were quick to respond and did so without using a canned response. The interaction was personalized to my unique situation.

- **Humanized brand:** Because their response wasn't a canned or automated "thanks!" it humanized their image for me. With one tweet, they went from a large, faceless company to a person who connected with me.

- **Stand out management:** Rachael did not have to wait a week to get approval to reach out to me or have to wait for direction to get out the right response. She acted immediately on behalf of the brand.

- **Inspired "wow":** They changed my perception of the brand, which had the long-term effect of causing me to choose Delta over other carriers each time I fly.

brands are usually minor; they represent a difference in message or theme of a channel. To be effective, differentiation needs to be holistic. It accounts not only for your presence but your interactions as well as your back-end management. The goal to truly be different impacts every aspect of your strategy and approach.

I agree with the *Wikipedia* definition of differentiation but in social media it's much more intense. The premise above is that differentiation is critical for competitors in a specific market.

> On social media, brands are not limited to competing with direct competitors. They are in a constant battle with every other brand on social networks competing for the attention of the audience.

In order to truly differentiate your brand on social media, six areas of your strategy need to be viewed holistically and in detail. Those areas are Presence, Paying Attention, Interaction, Content, Management, and Measurement. We will investigate these in more detail throughout the book and provide you with recommendations on how to implement and improve at each step.

IT'S ALL ABOUT POSITIONING

Blogger Sridhar Mutyala summarizes positioning in a blog post published in early 2011:

> Positioning was popularized by Al Ries and Jack Trout in their 1981 bestseller *Positioning: The Battle for Your Mind*. Their premise is that in an over-communicated world, consumers screen and reject much of the information being offered and only accept whatever matches their prior knowledge or experience.
> Businesses have to adapt to this environment by oversimplifying their message and by concentrating on narrow targets, the consumer segments that are most likely to listen and respond to their marketing. By focusing, businesses can hope to find some unoccupied space in a target consumer's set of perceptions and set up shop, if you will, at a safe distance from competitors.[2]

On social media the challenge of differentiation is particularly difficult, because everyone is on an equal playing field. In other words, it's extremely difficult to differentiate the look and feel of your overall social presence, because everyone is generally held to the same standard. Initially, all Facebook and Twitter pages look alike and are built on the same templates.

The key is to be distinctive in multiple areas. Your distinction needs to come not simply from your presence but also in how your brand organizes behind the scenes, including your approach to listening, interaction, content, management, and measurement.

Effective positioning on social media is about knowing what your brand stands for and embodying it on a regular basis. Companies known for their social media success are typically well positioned for service, and the quality interactions they have with their customers typically reverberate through the social media echo chamber, giving them more attention.

CASE STUDY   LEVI'S FRIENDS STORE

In April 2010 Levi's revamped their online shopping experience with the launch of the Levi's Friends Store. Visitors are encouraged to "Connect with Facebook" upon entering and, once connected, are delivered a personalized shopping experience, based on the likes and recommendations of friends.

A ClickZ article from 2010 describes the experience:

What's more, the Friends Store will be populated with merchandise that users and their friends can express interest in via Like button clicks. Levi's has placed a Like button next to every SKU, said Megan O'Connor, director of digital and social marketing.

"We really wanted to put [the Like button] as high up in the shopping path as possible," O'Connor said. "We feel like it's going to revolutionize the way people shop for jeans online. Everything from knowing other users' expressed preferences, to our brand ambassadors telling their friends through the Like functionality that these are their favorite jeans."[3]

This is a stand out approach to **social commerce**. Their ability to stand out is about creating a unique and memorable experience for their online customers. Levi's understands that the most effective and important advertising comes through the recommendation of friends. By applying this approach to their store, they are able to leverage these recommendations to drive sales directly on the site. This personalized experience leverages the dynamic content of Facebook and is personalized for each user.

Interested in learning more about **social commerce**? Head over to the Stand Out Social Marketing blog and check out this social commerce white paper from Awareness.

STANDING OUT IN GENERATION YOU

Being distinctive in the old broadcast marketing model was easier, because brands controlled the message. It's much more difficult in a dialog model, where the audience has more control. Social media gives businesses a way to communicate with their customers in a conversation that takes place where and when the audience wants to have it.

In 2007, *Time* magazine did something unprecedented by naming "You" person of the year. By "You" they meant all of us. The audience is in control, and that control is growing. Successful social media is about sharing the reins with the audience that is relevant to your world, and allowing the shared conversation to drive your bottom line.

Interested in learning just how fast social media is growing? An Infographic-published search engine journal titled ***The Growth of Social Media*** will give you a sense of just how fast social media is growing.

The power our audience has adds a new level of complexity to standing out. They are the publishers and they facilitate public conversations with brands directly. This means that part of a stand out strategy is having the ability to interact when they demand it. However, this challenge also presents a great opportunity that will change your approach to marketing.

A STAND OUT APPROACH TO MARKETING

Think about how you were trained to market. The campaign-centric vantage point of classic marketing teaches us to construct offers and messages that we wish to deliver and to broadcast them to our audience through a variety of channels (TV, Web, etc.). After the message is delivered, we wait and measure success in terms of responses. How many people responded to the offer? Did it generate a positive return on investment (ROI)?

The core of social media is the data available to marketers. That information, however, is only available through dialogs that are contextual. In other words, we can't rely on the traditional interruptive broadcast message to reach individuals. Finally, these conversations take place within communities, or social networks, and marketers need to recognize each social network's rules of engagement. While the rules are somewhat similar, they vary. For example, how you communicate on Twitter is different from how you communicate on Facebook or on YouTube.

To better illustrate this, let me give you an example of how this may look in practice. Let's say we decide to go into business selling shoes. Our marketing education and training would immediately inspire most of us to develop marketing plans based on traditional marketing principles. We would likely do market research on our target audience(s) and begin targeting broadcast messages at them across multiple channels, such as print, TV, and banner ads.

A distinctive approach on social media would have us develop a very different plan of attack. In this model, we would begin selling shoes by paying attention to conversations online. Some of them may be explicit "Anyone know where I can get a new pair of shoes at a good price?" Others may be implied "I have the annual office party next week, and I am not sure what to wear." Both cases give us windows into behaviors that indicate a higher likelihood to purchase shoes. Paying attention would drive interactions "Looking for a new outfit for the office party? How about some new shoes, too? Check these out." The conversation leads to higher sales conversions than a traditional approach, because we are able to target the individuals with the highest likelihood for results.

This new vantage point shifts the playing field. This is also why the principle of differentiation is so important on social media.

> With everyone vying to communicate within the social web, how can you rise above the noise?

SIX CHALLENGES OF SOCIAL MEDIA THAT AFFECT DIFFERENTIATION

Social media represents the biggest marketing opportunity and challenge ever faced by businesses. How we differentiate and how we manage this new way of interaction with consumers poses challenges that are common to businesses, regardless of size or industry. Many of these obstacles are the reason why so many companies have failed to find effective footing on the social web. Each of these challenges affects a brand's ability to stand out on social media.

1. INABILITY TO SCALE

The inability for organizations to scale—to quickly and easily manage, maintain, and measure multiple social channels—is a top theme at most businesses. This directly affects your ability to stand out on social media, because the back-end management of this presence impedes innovation.

Jeremiah Owyang of Altimeter Group recently published a blog post that discusses the **pain of scaling** social media programs in detail while breaking down the **social media management software** market.[4]

When asked how marketers will scale their social media marketing programs, the knee-jerk reaction from most market-ers is through people. This is ineffective, because scaling through individuals isn't a long-term solution. The challenge of scale in social media is both related to the growing number of channels available and the amount of content that needs to be syndicated across channels.

2. SECURITY AND CONTROL

Security and control is a business's ability to maintain multiple social media presences in a secure and manageable fashion while controlling how internal teams interface with their social audience. From small local operations to large multi-national enterprises, this is a critical concern as businesses adopt social media.

If you are looking for an example of a brand that has a great grasp on the control issue, look no further than Best Buy's Twelpforce initiative. There are multiple individuals tweeting and responding to customer-service issues on behalf of the brand, yet you would think they are all coming from one voice.

Without consistency and security there are real risks that exist around the way your social media presence is organized and managed. A lack of internal policies and control make it next to impossible to stand out.

3. LACK OF RESOURCES AND BUY-IN

Most businesses are operating in social media with an extreme lack of resources and next to no buy-in from senior executives. A contributing factor to this is the inability for most companies to develop meaningful reporting mechanisms (see the next point), but it is still shocking that social media has not been fully accepted in the highest levels of some of these enterprises.

Without executive-level support, developing a stand out approach is next to impossible. A well-managed and integrated social presence requires elevated thinking in order to engage with a broad view of the organization's overall marketing efforts. Without this, internal conflicts and roadblocks can limit a brand's ability to get the most out of its efforts in the social space.

Interested in learning how to **increase executive buy-in** for your social marketing? Check out a series of recent blog posts I published on the subject.

With that said, the only way to get resources through executive buy-in is to prove the value, which leads me to challenge number four.

4. REPORTING IS AD HOC

Reporting on social media is the single biggest hurdle faced by large organizations, because it affects every other area of a fine-tuned strategy. Without reporting, it is difficult to scale, get executive buy-in, maintain control, or centralize your social media program. What is surprising is that pulling general reports from the big channels—Facebook, Twitter, Flickr, YouTube—is a manual process on which people are spending a great deal of time. On this point there is a big hole to fill in around social media reporting. Organizations need a central place to collect data from multiple channels, simple ways to manipulate data to see how assets are performing, and to be able to assess which channels are providing the best bang for the buck.

Reporting that does not focus on the correct results leads to an approach that isn't focused on the correct goals. This makes a stand out program difficult to accomplish.

5. CENTRALIZATION

Organizations are looking to centralize social media efforts across the organization. A typical situation for most organizations is handling social media in silos. Different departments create pages and accounts for their divisions, and this makes it difficult to deploy a centralized strategy. For some large organizations this issue is on a global scale. Centralizing the social media strategy is something that is gaining a lot of momentum within large companies and most are moving to bring social media to one department that controls all engagement and interactions.

The biggest challenge for businesses grappling with the issue of centralization is behavior change. For most businesses social media started slowly. A few rogue or entrepreneurial employees began engaging in it, and it was not a centralized effort. When a centralized approach is implemented, behaviors need to change, and this can be an issue for businesses.

A company that does a great job at centralizing their strategy is JetBlue. From the top down the stated goal of social media is to improve the customer experience. Without a clear focus, standing out in social media is impossible.

6. OPERATING IN THE ECHO CHAMBER

In high school, basketball occupied 90 percent of my time. I played constantly, and when I wasn't playing, I was thinking about it and visualizing the game. Ken Pondelli, a local youth coach, gave me fantastic advice that I have since applied to nearly every aspect of my life. He explained that, to take my game to the next level, I needed to see it through the eyes of a coach. As a player, my experience was limited to playing my position; as a coach, I would see the game more holistically and fully begin to understand its nuances. What Ken was telling me was that I needed to shift my vantage point. I needed to see the game from a higher level to really comprehend it enough to improve. That small change led to an immediate improvement and success as a high-school player.

Differentiation in social media may seem close to impossible. The social media system operates as an echo chamber where the "biggest ideas" from the "most liked" and loudest personalities reverberate through its walls. When a well-liked and followed personality shares his or her opinion on the next big thing, brands follow like the Borg, to implement it without thinking through the consequences. Brands are competing in a landscape where similar ideas are echoed and, in turn, adopted by the masses, making it difficult to rise above the noise. As a part of this machine, it's impossible—or at best very difficult—to identify areas to differentiate. Similarly, it's impossible to be a sales leader, for example, if your view of the process is limited to the ground floor. In order to advance, it's necessary to view the sales department and vision for the business from a higher plain. In that case, your differentiator becomes the perspective from which you view sales.

BEING DIFFERENT

Right now you should be realizing that social media is, indeed, a different kind of beast. Not only is it a challenge to adapt your marketing to meet the needs of the social business paradigm brought on by the age of the Internet, it is also important to rise above the social media noise and differentiate yourself from the thousands of brands who are jumping into social media, all at the same time.

With that said, you should also be realizing that the obstacles to effective social media marketing can be overcome, and this will lead you to measurable results.

The most sophisticated marketers have managed to keep themselves ahead of the curve, and we can learn from the example they have set. Yet even then, while many have adopted social media as part of the marketing mix, the shift is so radical that many feel uneducated and overwhelmed by both the opportunities and challenges presented by social media. To cope with this as we move forward, I am going to ask you to do one thing: remove yourself from your role, the system, and begin viewing social media holistically. Become the coach, and view the space outside the echo chamber to identify the specific areas in your strategy that can be improved and differentiated. In this way, you can engage with an elevated view of what social media marketing can do for you, your company, and your industry.

ACTIONS AND TAKEAWAYS

- Make a list of all the social media channels your company is active on. Who owns and controls those channels? Are they unique, or are they similar to your competitors'? Is your company's unique selling proposition represented in your social presence?

- Outline your company's business objectives. For each, ask yourself whether social media can be a catalyst to help achieve those objectives. Elevate your vantage point, and look at your social marketing strategy holistically. Are you getting the most out of it in your opinion? Identify the two or three biggest challenges your company faces with regard to social marketing. With those identified, it will be much easier to pinpoint areas for improvement and outline strategies to enhance the current program.

CHAPTER 2

Stand Out by Paying Attention

Chris Brogan, social media strategist and best-selling author of *Trust Agents*, gave me some great advice a few years back. We were delivering a daylong social media workshop for Titleist and someone in the audience asked Chris what he believed to be the most important concept in social media. Chris paused a moment and responded, "It's not really about what you say, it's about what you hear and if you are paying attention."

This is the fundamental difference between traditional marketing efforts and social marketing. Traditionally, companies develop a message, broadcast it out to the world, and then listen to customer responses, communicated largely through sales. Now, to effectively market and sell through social media, brands must cultivate the ability to monitor and listen to what customers want, and *then* act on an effective marketing strategy. This simple message from Chris says it best: "pay attention first, interact later."

Paying attention is the heart of a brand's social media strategy. It's the ability of a brand to go beyond listening to deeply understanding the behaviors and motivations of the individuals it is communicating with. Deeper listening allows you to generate a knowledge base about your customers that is unique, thanks to social media, allowing you to apply your marketing efforts with more precision and direct intention. This act of deeper listening is *paying attention.* The good news for you is that brands that truly pay attention see dramatic results from their social media strategy. Let's jump right in with a decadently affordable example.

CASE STUDY FOILED CUPCAKES, PAYING ATTENTION
DRIVES CUPCAKE SALES ON TWITTER

Foiled Cupcakes is a Chicago-based company that sells cupcakes over the Internet. Surprisingly, they have no physical fully operating retail locations to date, and all products are sold directly online.

A blog post written by Brian Quinton for Entrepreneur.com in January 2011 describes a bit about the company and their approach to social media:

> Foiled fills about 1,000 dozen orders a month at an average cost of $38 each. But what's interesting is whom Foiled sells to. Founder and owner Mari Luangrath says 94 percent of her clientele was developed through leads received in social media, specifically Twitter.[1]

What struck me most about this story was Mari's approach. Instead of targeting individuals who were online talking specifically about which cupcakes to buy, she began communicating and relating to people within her target demographic (women ages 18–40) about something else she knew a lot about: shoes.

Quinton goes on to describe Mari's approach as "targeted listening." In other words, she identified the conversations that she could easily join in and be part of, thus developing relationships with her clientele and building her brand and business.

Here's how she goes about it: She engages in conversations with women who are on Twitter talking about shoes they had bought or are planning to buy. Mari gives advice, compliments different purchases, and in doing so, develops a community of new interactions around something she is genuinely interested in. By engaging in a community with a specific intention, and being open about her business, her interactions often generate cupcake sales for her business.

HOW FOILED CUPCAKES PAYS ATTENTION

Paying attention is more than watching for keywords that are immediately related to the sale you want to make. Mari pays attention to the individuals that make up her target market and develops relationships with them based on common interests. She knows her market, she's interested in her market, and she cares about how her product fits into the lives of her customers overall. By knowing that her consumer base has an affinity for shoes, Mari is able to develop relationships that lead to sales, allowing her business to succeed in a unique way relative to her competitors, and completely online.

A strategy based on paying attention is about intimately understanding the people in your target market and what they care about. It is also an action-oriented, data-driven strategy. It implies that the results will lead to some form of action, based on data gathered during the conversation. These data come from a lot of different places, including the conversation itself, the profiles of the individuals you are paying attention to, and the history of the person or people you are paying attention to. To start, we need to determine whom you want to listen to and how to start paying attention to the things they say about the issues you care about.

PAYING ATTENTION MADE EASY

Identifying your purpose in social media is the first step to finding the right conversations to be a part of. As part of a 2010 survey conducted by Awareness, Inc., over 300 brands that were engaged in social media were asked how they use social networks.[2] They responded with the following:

- 78 percent identify and respond to customer-service issues.

- 64 percent identify individuals looking for my product or service.

- 38 percent identify individuals who influence sales of my product or service.

- 17 percent identify behaviors associated with people who are likely to buy my product or service.

When asked if they have a formal tracking process in place to manage these processes and better understand success criteria, only 18 percent said "yes." Of the 82 percent that said "no," 78 percent indicated they are looking to implement new processes and tools to track social conversations better. Building the bridge between identifying your role online and managing interactions at a scalable level isn't as difficult as it seems. Trust me. Once we get you there, the ability to pay attention is easy as pie. The first step is to establish a listening system and develop useful information.

CASE STUDY DELTA AIRLINES, CUSTOMER SERVICE EVOLVED WITH @DELTAASSIST

Remember my friend Rachael Rensink from Chapter 1? I followed up with her while writing this book, and it turns out that a lot has changed for Delta over the last 12 months.

She explains how easy it can be to monitor, respond, and fulfill your company's purpose on social media:

> I think that when you talk about listening, you think of complexity. To me, the biggest component to listening is actually paying attention. That's all I did when you and I first met. I pulled up your profile, and it was the data in that profile—who you were and everything else—that I paid attention to. Your profile showed that you had a new baby, and I was pregnant at the time, and my immediate response was "Hey, I relate to that. I relate to you." And remember, I am "the brand."

Delta's social media program has changed dramatically since I was first acquainted with it back in 2010. Rachael and her team have implemented the @DeltaAssist program specifically to pay attention to customer service issues. They have increased their social media staff to fourteen, and they have developed sophisticated processes to manage relationships with customers. A cornerstone of their strategy has been paying attention. Yet the implementation of their strategy was only effective when synchronized with the clear set of goals that the company felt it could achieve through social media. Rachael's early outreach set the tone for the type of listening and interactions that would grow with the company's social media strategy overall.

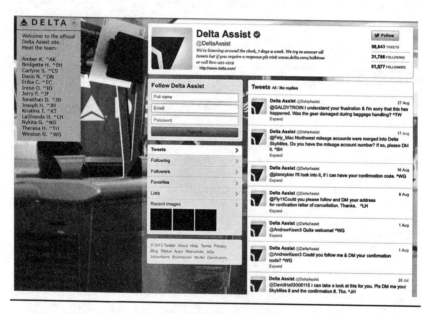

In this same fashion it is important for you to target your purpose early on, listen to relevant conversations, and determine who within your company is ready to take the lead. The following provides step-by-step advice about how to set up your listening program.

While my experiences with Delta have been outstanding, they have had a few social media challenges. If you are interested in learning more about some of the public issues they have faced and, more important, their outstanding responses to them, jump over to my blog and search for Delta.

PAYING ATTENTION: THE BASICS

STEP 1: ATTENTION OUTPOSTS: IDENTIFYING WHERE THE CONVERSATIONS ARE HAPPENING

Where to pay attention is different for every company. Begin the process of identifying which social outposts to participate in by implementing a very broad strategy. Don't focus on Facebook and Twitter alone. Go beyond the obvious platforms as well, which will allow you to identify a whole world of conversations that may be relevant to your business.

As you collect data, you will start to see where the most relevant conversations are occurring, giving you deeper insight into the social spaces you should participate in first.

The audience for each company is very different, and they all tend to gravitate toward different social media destinations. For some, the destination is Facebook or Twitter, for others it might be blogs or LinkedIn. It's difficult for you to know without taking a moment to observe the social media space and understanding your market.

WWE SOCIAL MARKETING

World Wrestling Entertainment (WWE) has been active in social media since the early days (around 2008). In that time, their brand has grown to become one of the most well-differentiated and exciting destinations on the social web.

Here are some of WWE's highly impressive social media stats:

- WWE superstar John Cena is the seventh-most "Liked" and followed athlete on Facebook and Twitter (in terms of total following). Eight WWE superstars are among the top fifty most liked and followed athletes (Fan Page Lists http://fanpagelist.com/category/athletes/view/list/sort/fans/page1).

- WWE is the second-most followed sports brand in the world, just behind the NBA (Fan Page Lists http://fanpagelist.com/category/brands/sports/).

- WWE manages hundreds of Facebook and Twitter accounts for their promotions, superstars, personalities, company, and events.

Their social media success is staggering, but it wasn't always this way. WWE jumped into social media in 2008 by launching WWE Universe, an online community where fans could connect and chat. The site saw instant success, with over a million registered users. With such a passionate and vocal audience, WWE expected high engagement rates, but that didn't quite happen. I had the chance to connect with Mark Keys, former Vice President, Interactive Content Production and Social Media at WWE (and currently the Vice President, Web Content and Operations at FUSE Networks), and he summed it up by explaining that ". . . after all those people joined, we only had a fraction of them engaging on a daily basis."

WWE Universe continued until 2010, when Keys and his team decided it was time to join the fans who were participating on other social networks. They migrated their focus to Facebook and Twitter, the two destinations with the most active WWE fans. Then, within about thirteen months, they experienced 600 percent growth, jumping from one page to over a hundred managed pages, and the fan base grew from 250,000 to over 38 million.

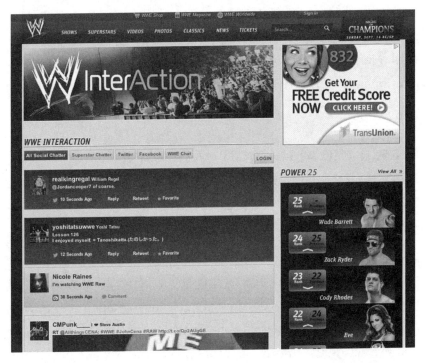

Today WWE is continuing their staggering growth in social media. Superstars live tweet during events, and it's extremely common for WWE-related Twitter hashtags to top the trending list on Twitter during their weekly television shows.

WWE personality and movie star Dwayne "The Rock" Johnson often tries to get specific terms to trend on Twitter during his appearances on WWE TV. Want to learn more? Head over to the blog and search for **#Boots2Asses**.

Selecting the right destinations to participate in from the beginning is critical for every brand. As in the WWE case study, even with a large audience, it was critical for them to focus on the destinations where they will be heard, where interaction will be highest, and where opportunities for engagement will continue to grow.

STEP 2: THE ATTENTION MATRIX AND ATTENTION SILOS: PAYING ATTENTION TO THE RIGHT CONVERSATIONS

The process of paying attention starts by identifying keywords, phrases, and individuals that are relevant to your business. From the people in your audience talking specifically about your brand to those talking about your industry or your competitors, paying attention is about harnessing the conversations that matter most and extracting the information that helps you decide how, where, and when to engage with your community. The example in Table 2.1 uses the brand *Pella Windows* to demonstrate how keywords and categories can be outlined for effective monitoring on the social web. Table 2.1 is an example of an Attention Matrix.

To arrive at a set of strategic keywords, Pella Windows needs to understand the words associated with its product or service domain, industry classifications, and associated customer pain points. To get this list of keywords they would start by talking with their sales team to get a sense of the terms and pain/passion

Table 2.1 **Attention Matrix Example: Pella Windows**

Area	Examples
Brand	Pella
Products	Casement, awning, double-hung, bay windows, sliding windows, vinyl windows, wood windows
Product domain	Windows, window replacement, home improvement, home additions
Industry	Home improvement, home construction, home remodeling
Associated customer problems	Broken windows, drafts, high energy bills, more home space, expanding family
Competitors	Andersen, NewPro
Associated buying	Doors, insulation, weather stripping
Retail/distribution	Home Depot, Lowes

points used in their conversations with prospects and customers, gather competitive intelligence or speak directly with their customers. Once the keywords are identified, Pella Windows can:

- Pay attention to keywords across multiple social media platforms—Facebook, Twitter, blogs, forums, as well as all major search engines.

- Analyze keyword popularity and relevancy, and select the keywords that tie in best to the company's social marketing goals.

- Allocate social media resources to drive desired outcomes:

  - If driving higher brand awareness within the home improvement category is a stated goal, Pella may opt to put more resources toward monitoring "home improvement" mentions.

- If focusing on sales, Pella would monitor behavioral- and pain-focused keywords that are associated with buying.

- If focusing on service, Pella would focus on conversations that are associated with typical points of customer frustration, in an effort to resolve issues before they become bigger issues.

Now, the conversations on the social web are continuous and overwhelming. Sifting through the noise and paying attention to the conversations that matter most means that you need to get organized as you embark on this long-term strategy. Using the attention matrix similar to the Pella Windows example can help, providing you a way to categorize your efforts and move your team forward. So let's turn the focus on to you.

Your approach to paying attention will center around identifying conversations that relate five areas (1) *Your Company and Brand* (2) *Your Market Landscape* (3) *The Competition* (4) *The Influencers* and *(5) Buying Intent.* These are your attention silos. Let's take a moment to dig in and investigate each silo in more detail.

Your Company and Brand

The purpose is to understand whether or not people are talking about you, who is talking about you, and where they are talking about you. You'll need to list as many company- and brand-related keywords as possible and begin paying attention to them immediately. As you start to dig into the conversations around these terms you'll get insight into who is talking about you, how they are talking about you, what their sentiment is around your brand, and other topics they discuss when you are mentioned.

Market Landscape

Paying attention to your market gives you the data you need to understand the larger sphere in which you operate. By going beyond the conversations about your company, this elevated view gives you the ability to better understand trends, hot-button topics, and key issues within your market segment as they evolve.

Here are some questions you can ask to identify market-related keywords and phrases:

- What are some of the buzzwords associated with your industry?
- Are there particular phrases that are associated with your market?
- What are the keywords and categories that define your market?

This exercise will keep you on top of the relevant conversations occurring in your industry and allow you to modify your messaging to fit market demand.

The Competition

Paying attention to competitors will give you the competitive intelligence you need to understand their vision and how they view the market. It can tell you what other companies they are working with and provide insight into the companies they are trying to attract.

You will come to understand their direction in the market, trends they feel are important to focus on, whom they engage with, and what they are offering the market. Most important, you will start to gain insight into how you are *different* from your competitors. This will influence your marketing messages and ongoing communication to that same market. Finally, you will gain insight into your intended brand perception versus your actual brand perception. For example, you may believe that the market views you as the "high quality" alternative, when, in fact, they actually see you as the "high value" alternative. Subtle difference, I know, but it is extremely important as you craft your messaging.

The Influencers

This is all about generating a deeper understanding of what your industry's influencers are saying. Influencers are the pundits of your market. It's critical for your business to understand what these individuals are talking about, whom are they talking to, and which issues excite them most.

What to pay attention to:

- An influencer list
- Their specific blogs and Twitter feeds
- The blogs on their blogroll and individuals that interact with them regularly on their blog, Twitter, and Facebook.

Begin by identifying influencers using a tool such as Klout or Twittalyzer. You will want to generate not only a list of general influencers in social media but also a list of influencers of specific topics relevant to your business and industry.

Buying Intent

This is where paying attention becomes really important. Measuring and understanding buying intent can be extremely tricky, but it can pay huge dividends when executed correctly. Paying attention is used specifically to identify conversations in which one or more of the participants is expressing intent to buy a product or service that you offer. The words and phrases you listen for will vary by industry, and they need to be vetted based on previous buying patterns. To illustrate this point let's use a specific example. Let's say we run the social marketing team at Jeep. Our objective is to generate leads on the web and filter those leads to local dealers.

We have to start by imagining the types of conversations people searching for a new car might have over the social web:

- "Test-drive Jeep"

- "Jeep recommendations"

- "Jeep dealerships in (state, city)"

- "New Jeep"

The example above provides a specific brand name—Jeep. We could get more specific—Jeep Grand Cherokee—or more broad, by substituting the type of vehicle (SUV) or the market. The point is that we are trying to identify specific individuals with whom we can have dialog, because we know they are expressing a higher likelihood of purchasing our product.

Developing and managing these attention silos focuses your strategy and allows you to pay attention to the right places. Within these buckets you should identify specific categories. This will help you organize and prioritize individual conversations, as well as help you identify specific groups of individuals for follow-up. Below are some generic categories, and they should be enhanced to meet the needs of your company:

- Sales—Sales-related conversations.

- Service—Customer service–related issues.

- Product—Areas to help improve the product or offering.

- Questions—General questions about our business.

- Compliment—Praise for your company.

Brands that accomplish this are able to identify new sales opportunities, as well as customer service issues, as they arise, as was the case with Salesforce.com in 2006.

CASE STUDY SALESFORCE.COM, "THE FORCE,"
PAYS ATTENTION

Customers look to Salesforce.com to maintain important sales information that is critical to their business. In 2006, a series of service interruptions caused an uproar among users when the system went offline and could not be accessed.

A ZDNet article from February 1, 2006 summarizes the situation:

Several disgruntled users took their complaints to the blogosphere after enduring the series of outages, including one that reportedly knocked portions of the site offline for several hours. Several customers went as far as to set up blogs, including one "for frustrated users of Salesforce.com," called GripeForce.

"This is starting to happen all too often," the GripeForce blogger wrote in the site's first blog post on January 30, 2006. "From 10:30 a.m. through lunch, Salesforce was down. This is too much. Two days left in the month, and the sales team can't access their data."[3]

Salesforce realized that open communication was the heart of the issue for complaining customers. They wanted more transparency in what was happening. They wanted to know that Salesforce knew of the outage and was in the process of correcting it.

The response to the customer complaints came from Salesforce in less than two months with the announcement of Trustforce, a site dedicated to providing up-to-date information on the status of Salesforce and, if necessary, communication on what they were doing to rectify any issues.

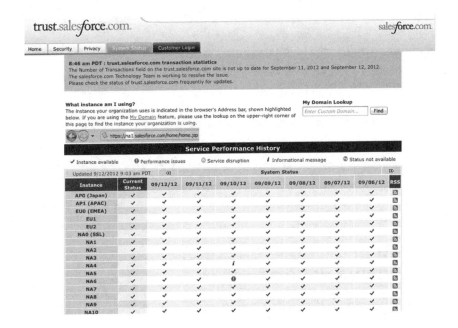

Salesforce built Trustforce-based feedback from users in direct response to the critical blog coverage around outages. In the words of Salesforce, *Trust starts with transparency.*

The site provides:

- Live and historical data on system performance.

- Up-to-the minute information on planned maintenance.

- Phishing, malicious software, and social engineering threats.

- Best security practices for your organization.

- Information on how we safeguard your data.

WHY TRUSTFORCE IS IMPORTANT

1. **Salesforce paid attention to their customers**. Listening would have identified the specific customers with issues. Paying attention allowed them to get to the root of the issue, which was customers wanted more communication from Salesforce.

2. **They spoke with customers**. Before launching Trustforce, Salesforce took the time to meet with customers and formulate a plan to meet their needs.

3. **Full transparency**. As part of Trustforce, they provide a grid with up-to-the minute information on how servers are performing. This level of transparency lets customers know exactly when and if there are any issues with the service.

STEP 3: ATTENTION TRACKING: MEASURING YOUR PROGRAM

Look for common themes to include in future programs. Capturing key conversations and themes is easier than most companies think. Getting the data and pulling out common themes and hot-button issues can help differentiate your overall strategy.

While paying attention there are several things you should look at in detail and track on an ongoing basis including:

- Mentions

- Brand sentiment

- Volume of conversations

- Share of voice

- Competitive comparison

The solutions can be varied, depending on where these issues surface and how they are best addressed, given your type of business and resources. Twitter was a key tool for Delta and might be for you as well. Or perhaps monitoring and listening to customer conversations on social media will help you gather the information you need to deliver an internally managed online platform that solves your customer issues, as it did for Salesforce.com in 2006. Either way, what to do with all this information is exactly where your judgment as a mover and shaker in your industry comes into play. The tools and approaches presented here show you how to generate that information. From here, you can take a new perspective on your market and determine with new resolve the role you want to take in your market and how you can take advantage of these new kinds of information and feedback. Now, having developed your basic approach, you are ready to take it to the next level and build a deeper strategy that is focused beyond the conversations and onto behaviors.

ACTIONS AND TAKEAWAYS

- Build an attention matrix to help focus on specific keywords that you will pay attention to.

- Develop a list of keywords in each of the attention silos. Ask other stakeholders in your company to develop their own lists. Use these different perspectives to find new destinations for establishing your presence.

- Identify terms to better understand buying intent. Start by looking into recent sales and investigating what important topics were discussed leading up to a transaction.

- Investigate how your competitors are viewed in social media. Use this knowledge to start thinking about how you see your business can be set apart from the pack!

CHAPTER 3

Stand Out by Paying Attention to Behaviors

Paying attention to behaviors means understanding the behaviors that your audience displays, based on the conversations they are having and the actions they are taking. These data are used to predict the next actions of your audience. Through identifying behaviors, demonstrated pains and praises, and criteria that indicate a higher likelihood to buy, you can begin to build a correlate of the social conversations you are paying attention to and a return on your investment. Similar to the Foiled Cupcakes example, paying attention to behaviors is about listening to the social web to identify the individuals who are demonstrating a propensity to buy your product or service, based on their actions and conversations.

In this phase we will dig deeper into paying attention to behaviors by exploring the concepts of hyper-targeting, social nurturing, and social scoring. Implemented correctly, these tactics will help your brand to stand out and drive bottom-line gains.

CASE STUDY TRINET IS LISTENING FOR CHANGE

On his blog, Umberto Milletti, CEO of InsideView, offered an excellent example of paying attention for a B2B company called **TriNet**.

TriNet is a successful and rapidly growing HR services firm that delivers payroll HR compliance to small and mid-size businesses. TriNet has found that talking to prospects at times of change (for example, with new CEO/management, new funding, expansion, significant changes in hiring) critically drives their sales team's success. Timely and in-depth knowledge of trigger events at their target accounts gives them compelling reasons to start conversations. *With an incredible 70 percent conversion-to-appointment rate, TriNet has experienced substantial success.*[1]

At conferences and events I am often asked to provide B2B examples of social media success, and in my opinion, TriNet is an excellent case study. What I like most about TriNet is that they paid attention to very specific behaviors, knowing that these events represented a higher likelihood of sales conversion.

Change is a common compelling event that leads to a purchase. Milletti says, "Certain trigger events, such as leadership changes, new product launches, new office openings, or mergers and acquisitions, can lead to buying opportunities for new products or services." Social media adds a new dimension to understanding these changes as they occur, in real time. Harnessing social data to capture these insights and details can be the driver that increases sales significantly.

WHAT TO PAY ATTENTION TO

What actions or events signal a buying decision in your customer base? Do you understand the sales and marketing cycle enough to identify those events and apply that knowledge to converting more sales? When you can figure this out, your conversion rates will skyrocket.

The key to doing this well is understanding the behaviors and intentions that are typically associated with a specific outcome. This is *hyper-targeting*.

HYPER-TARGETING

Hyper-targeting is the ability to target an individual (or individuals) who displays a specific set of behaviors that indicate a likelihood of buying. It's not about broadcasting a message to a specific demographic, but rather to an individual. It's an important concept to grasp, so let's start by giving you an example of how you can accomplish it on both a micro and macro scale.

HYPER-TARGETING MARATHON RUNNERS

A well-known shoe retailer had gathered enough data to know that runners were more likely to buy new running shoes roughly three months before a marathon. With this knowledge, the company would typically run banner ads on sites like *Runner's World* and *ESPN Magazine* three to five months before a race. They believed that the conversions to sales would be much higher, because of the targeting and timing of the advertising.

The marketing team quickly realized that, while response rates through the banners were good, they could be far better. In an effort to improve conversions, the team began concentrating efforts on finding marathoners who were blogging and tweeting about their training programs three to five months before a marathon. When a runner would get into that "buying window," the retailer would interact with him or her in a supportive, meaningful, and "non-salesy" way.

Implementing this approach caused conversion rates to improve by more than five times over banner advertising, and spending on traditional media declined sharply, vastly improving the company's overall return on investment (ROI). These results came about because they were able to hyper-target the individuals that had the highest likelihood of buying running shoes.

Let's apply this concept on a more micro-level. Once you have the data on typical buying behaviors, you can become much more detailed about to whom and where you pay attention. In turn, you can develop a hyper-targeting program designed specifically to achieve a desired outcome.

Again, let's refer to the running shoes company as an example. Buying data are mined and trends are unveiled, indicated by behavioral patterns of people who are likely to buy. With this information a buyer's likely "path to purchase" is outlined. See Table 3.1.

With these data, it becomes easier to direct offers specifically to runners through social media and other marketing vehicles, all in order to drive increased conversions.

The marketing program would look something like that shown in Table 3.2.

Table 3.1 **Sample Path to Purchase**

Timing	Behavior
12–9 months out	Runners begin blogging and tweeting about their marathon training programs
9–6 months out	Tweets and blog posts continue; 19% of those followed joining the Marathon Runner's group on Facebook
6–3 months out	Runners begin looking for new shoes and other equipment. They spend time researching specific sites to enhance their training regimens.
3 months out	Purchase new running sneakers

Table 3.2 **Sample Path to Purchase Marketing Actions**

Timing	Behavior	Marketing action
12–9 months out	Runners begin blogging and tweeting about their marathon training programs	Identify bloggers and tweeters; begin dialog with them and continue throughout the process. Provide tips and suggestions on the next steps in their training programs
9–6 months out	Tweets and blog posts continue; 19% of those followed joining the Marathon Runner's group on Facebook	Continue dialog; begin running traditional advertising. Build trust and rapport with them by providing suggestions on how to train and provide online resources to assist their online training regimens
6–3 months out	Runners begin looking for new shoes and other equipment. They spend time researching specific sites to enhance their training regimens	Suggest purchase throughout the process to assist in their training through social channels

Table 3.2 **Sample Path to Purchase Marketing Actions** *(continued)*

3 months out	Purchase new running sneakers.	Individually offer specials or discounts to create incentive to purchase

Hyper-targeting requires a deep understanding of the buying behaviors of your audience. In order to accomplish this, you can implement a scoring and nurturing system over social media to collect profile information and monitor behaviors.

To best uncover the typical path to purchase for your company, start by looking at the actions taken by recent buyers prior to purchase. Understand all marketing interactions, site visits, and behaviors taken leading up to the event. For deeper intelligence, spend time with your sales team to better understand what common behaviors they identify with hot prospects.

Want to dig deeper on Social Scoring? Head over to the blog and search for Social Prospecting and Social Scoring for helpful articles, blog posts, and cases on the subject.

LISTENING FOR LEADS,
PAYING ATTENTION GENERATES
MILLIONS FOR IBM

Often, when you think of companies doing innovative things in social media, you think about smaller more nimble companies. A recent blog post on eMarketer featured an interview with Ed Linde II of IBM who discussed the IBM rollout and success of a program called "Listening for Leads."

Linde explains the program and discusses the outcomes of the program below, from an interview with eMarketer:

> We also have a program called Listening for Leads, where we have people we call "seekers" who on a voluntary basis go to particular social media sites where they listen to conversations and determine whether there's a potential sales opportunity.
>
> Seekers listen to and look at conversations. For example, if someone says, "I'm looking to replace my old server" or "Does anyone have any recommendations on what kind of storage device will work in this type of situation?" or "I'm about to issue a RFP; does anyone have a sample RFP I could work from?" Those are all pretty good clues that someone's about to buy something or start the buying process.
>
> We have uncovered millions of dollars' worth of sales leads through our intelligent listening program, and we've closed a lot of business, and we expect to do more.[2]

This is an excellent example of B2B listening, featuring one of the largest and most respected brands in the world. While IBM may have a greater ability to fund experimental programs like Listening for Leads, their approach is simple. Seekers go on a voluntary basis and pay attention to people who are expressing specific buying behaviors. When this happens they are routed to the appropriate sales representative for follow-up.

WHAT TO PAY ATTENTION TO

Who in your company is paying attention? Could you have a subset of your company "search" for leads to share with the sales team? Imagine your entire company engaged in identifying sales prospects for your products and services during downtime. This could generate a significant impact on your bottom line, as you identify more and more sales-ready prospects.

SOCIAL NURTURING AND SOCIAL SCORING

Those of you familiar with marketing automation systems likely understand the concept of nurturing and scoring. Lead nurturing programs aim to help guide prospects down a specific path, based on specific behaviors they have demonstrated. Lead scoring is a method of assigning points to each prospect based on specific criteria you set—those attributes you've identified as being most often associated with serious prospective customers. The higher the scores, the more likely they're the right target prospects that are actively engaged in the buying process. Nurturing and scoring allow marketers to bucket groups of prospects together and serve marketing messages to them at the right time of their buying process. Typically, this is a business-to-business marketing concept, but it can be easily transferred to a business-to-consumer model as well. The scores assigned to individuals are the basis for the campaigns you run against them.

The most accurate lead scoring models comprise both explicit and implied information.

- **Explicit scores** are based on information provided by or about the prospect; for example, company size, industry segment, job title, or geographic location.

- **Implied scores** are derived from monitoring prospect behavior; examples of these include website visits, white paper downloads, or e-mail opens and clicks.

This approach is perfect for social media, where the system is based on behaviors and conversations that can easily be scored. That said, there is a reason why not every company has implemented this approach yet. Lead nurturing and scoring systems are based on a very basic premise: *that you know who the person is before he or she enters the program.* That can be a huge challenge in social media, where matching profiles across networks is difficult. To be truly effective, you need to know that Prospect A on Facebook is the same person as @ProspectA on Twitter, and so on for each network. Details on resolving this issue are addressed in more detail in the next chapter under the heading "Profiling Your Social Audience," but the basis of the approach is to have a database and system in place that allows you to track activities of potential buyers before they enter your system. In fact, they may not even know your brand as you begin paying attention to them.

Let me give you an example of how this looks in practice, again using the running shoe example.

- **April 2011:** Randy Craig announces to his friends on his blog, Facebook page, and Twitter account that he is running in the 2013 Boston Marathon and will begin training immediately.

  - ACTION: Capture Randy's public profile information in our monitoring and CRM systems. In our system he gets +5 points for announcing he will be running. We begin to actively monitor his streams and activity across the web. In addition, we begin to engage with him.

- **August 2011:** Through our prompting, Randy joins our Marathon Training group on Facebook. He is actively engaged and begins creating relationships with others who will also be running in the Marathon.

  - ACTION: Randy gets an additional +10 points, and we continue regular outreach.

- **September 2011:** Again through our prompting, Randy signs up for our weekly newsletter "Marathon Training Tips."

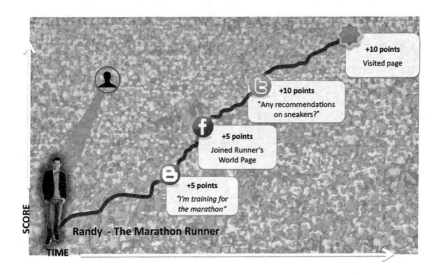

- ACTION: Randy is now a part of our database. He gets an additional +10 points.

- **January 2012:** Randy hit a minimum lead score and receives an e-mail inviting him to purchase shoes and equipment at a 10 percent discount to help him on the big day. He buys, and life is good.

This is an example of hyper-targeting and social scoring in practice. It may seem like a daunting task, but below are the steps you need to follow to pay attention to behaviors for your brand.

A THREE-STEP PROCESS FOR PAYING ATTENTION TO BEHAVIORS

1. Identify Relevant Data and Behaviors

The running shoes example is straightforward. It's based on data already possessed by the brand that allowed them to build out a more detailed process in social media. Begin by outlining the behaviors of recent sales. To do this, make sure you are capturing relevant details from new sales, Twitter account, Facebook account, blog address, etc. Gather this all together and do some reconnaissance. Detail out the buyer's activity over the last few months (where available) and attempt to match up similarities. This will be manual at first.

Match these data up with data from your CRM system, marketing automation tool, or from a monitoring tool that you own.

2. Invest in Infrastructure

Investigate and understand your market by implementing tools to help coordinate your efforts. You should look at tools in four categories—monitoring, social marketing management, CRM, and marketing automation. It's critical that data are shared among these systems, so you have a solid idea of how a buyer progresses through the entire process. Table 3.3 shows some tools to investigate in each category, as well as tools that accomplish all three functions.

Table 3.3 is by no means a comprehensive list. At last count there were over 300 vendors in the monitoring space alone, and price points ranged from free to *extremely* expensive. Before investing considerable time and money in a more robust solution, I recommend getting started with some of the less expensive tools, until you have your baseline data accumulated.

Need to know what questions to ask as you evaluate vendors? Awareness recently published **"The Social Marketing Management Checklist,"** a guide to helping businesses figure out which solutions work best for their businesses.

Table 3.3 Sample List of Vendors in Each Category

CRM	Marketing automation	SMMS	Listening
Salesforce.com	Marketo	Awareness Social Marketing Hub	Radian6
NetSuite	Eloqua	Sprout	Sysomos
Oracle	Pardot	Spredfast	Alterian SDL
	Genius.com	Hootsuite	

Interested in **Social Marketing Automation**? I recently published a blog post with a detailed infographic that defines the market and what you should be looking for in a social marketing automation software package.

Some free monitoring tools to consider include (note all descriptions provided were taken from the providers' websites):

- **Social Mention** (www.socialmention.com): Social Mention is a social media search and analysis platform that aggregates user-generated content from across the online universe into a single stream of information. It allows you to easily track and measure what people are saying about you, your company, a new product, or any topic across the web's social media landscape in real time. Social Mention monitors over a hundred social media properties directly, including: Twitter, Facebook, FriendFeed, YouTube, Digg, Google, and more.

- **BlogPulse** (www.blogpulse.com): BlogPulse is an automated trend-discovery system for blogs. BlogPulse applies machine-learning and natural-language processing techniques to discover trends in the highly dynamic world of blogs.

- **Google Alerts** (alerts.google.com): Google Alerts are e-mail updates of the latest relevant Google results (web, news, etc.) based on your choice of query or topic. Enter the topic you wish to monitor, then click preview to see the type of results you'll receive. Some handy uses of Google Alerts include:

- monitoring a developing news story

- keeping current on a competitor or industry

- getting the latest on a celebrity or event

- keeping tabs on your favorite sports teams

• **Twitter-specific monitoring tools**: There are a ton of free Twitter monitoring tools available. Some of the more notable ones are listed below (all summaries were taken from each tools "About" page):

- **Monitter** is a real-time Twitter search tool that enables you to monitor a set of keywords on Twitter. It also allows you to narrow the search to a particular geographic location, allowing you to find out what's going on in a particular part of the world.

- **Twazzup** gives you real-time news for a specific subject and delivers that information from websites and Twitter. It also provides a list of recent influencers on a specific topic.

- **Pulse of the Tweeters.** Users on twitter often talk about common topics. Twitter calls these "trends" and identifies the top trending topics in real time. As Twitter continues to grow, it becomes more and more difficult for a new user to figure out the difference between useful content and spam. Pulse of the Tweeters provides a trend-specific ranking of users that is able to identify the most influential users across each topic. By using their ranking scheme, it is easy to identify the trendsetters and the tweets that matter most.

- **MentionMap** is an exciting web app for exploring your Twitter network. Discover which people interact the most and what they're talking about. It's also a great way to find relevant people to follow.

- **Twitalyzer** knows who is in your social network, and we know where they live, allowing you to be more targeted in your outreach efforts.

3. Develop Your Scoring Methodology and Categorization

Building out your scoring methodology is based on the data you uncover in the first two steps. This is going to be a fluid process that will evolve over time. After getting the appropriate tools in place, start by giving points for the bigger behaviors (or events) that an individual takes, like joining a specific group on Facebook or replying directly to one of your tweets.

There are 3 things to consider as you build this portion of the program:

1. **Social profile score.** This represents the total of all scores and actions accumulated for a specific social profile you are tracking. Scoring tallies should reflect lead demographics and behavior such as:

   a. Specific tweets—mentioning specific keywords and phrases

   b. Joining specific groups

   c. Blogging

   d. Demographic details (title, etc.)

   e. Influence score (Klout score, etc.)

   f. Visiting your site

Compile a grid that accounts for all measurable social actions and apply associated scores to each action. Your grid may look something like the example in Table 3.4. It's important to note that that grid represents only social behaviors. Don't forget to account for other non-social behaviors as you complete this grid (website visits, form completions, etc.)

2. **Social profile half-life.** If your lead hasn't been active within a certain time frame, you may want to deduct points from his or her score to indicate a lack of engagement. For example, an individual with a high score that has not expressed a buying behavior in more than two weeks would be deducted 15 points. He or she would no longer be classified as "hot" and would therefore receive a different stream of marketing offers.

Table 3.4 **Calculating Your Social Profile Score**

Action	Score	Category
Tweeted with specific keywords	+1	B
Tweeted with corporate account	+2	E
Joined Facebook group	+5	H
Blog post on specific subject	+10	A
Blog post comment	+5	V
Klout score between 1 and 20 and influential on subject	+5	I
Klout score above 40 and influential on subject	+7	O
Commented on LinkedIn group	+5	R
		A
		L

CHAPTER 4

Stand Out Interactions

If paying attention is the "yin" of social media, interaction is the "yang." You can't have a balanced and effective social media strategy without both. Together, they make it work. Interaction defines how you communicate with your audience, as well as how you encourage them to engage with your brand and content. To stand out, you need to ensure that the interactions you prompt are meaningful and remarkable from the perspective of your client base.

In the first two chapters we discussed how paying attention is an "active function." From the beginning, we know that some sort of action needs to be taken, based on what is being heard (or overheard). Now we can look at the terms of the interaction that follows paying attention and how that engagement shapes the relationship that the participants in the space have toward each other. That includes you. I hope you will come to see that interaction is a dual-purpose act. It requires responding to other people's content and conversing with people who are interacting with your content.

There are three components of interaction we will be investigating in the next three chapters. The first deals with how you engage with your audience, the second deals with the science behind interactions, and the third deals with tactics and strategies aimed at getting your audience to engage with your brand and content. Taken together these components are critical to a stand out social media strategy.

BUILDING INTERACTION

Interacting with your audience is likely one of the main reasons your social media program was started. Interaction goes beyond having a casual conversation. It involves understanding the *where, how,* and *why* that something is happening, and increasing its effectiveness and frequency across channels, and it is vital to program success. Whom you engage with, what you say, and how they respond, will influence your overall brand perception.

IS ANYONE REALLY LISTENING TO YOUR MESSAGES?

You might have 50,000 Twitter followers or 5,000 Facebook fans, but are they really interacting with and listening to you?

- What can you learn about that audience that can help you focus your message?
- Where are they interacting and engaging?
- What questions are they asking and what are they talking about?
- What are their individual social profiles?

Your approach to interaction will follow four steps:

1. **Where are they?** Determining where the conversations are happening.

2. **Look who's talking:** Understanding the individuals who are communicating.

3. **What's the context?** Understanding what the conversation is about and why it is occurring.

4. **How to interact:** Mapping out interaction strategies.

STEP ONE: DETERMINE WHERE IT'S HAPPENING

The people you could potentially engage with fall in two categories, those in "observed" conversations and those in "facilitated" conversations. Observed conversations involve people you have overheard talking on social networks about subjects that are relevant to your business. This category could include all of the types of conversations outlined in the paying attention chapter. If you run a local coffee shop, you may hear a conversation between two friends discussing good places to get together. You want to join that conversation, as it relates to your business. The point to remember here is that these are conversations outside of those that you or your brand initiated.

Facilitated conversations include all the conversations your brand initiates. These are through the same channels outlined above, but they are started by your brand. For example, your brand posts a blog entry about a hot topic in your industry. The comments you receive on that post were the result of you facilitating the conversation. Keep this in mind, because the type of engagement and the interactions that follow will be affected by whether or not you initiate the conversation or are joining another conversation already in progress.

As you look at your possible world of interactions, consider that activity can vary from one platform to the next. It is important to not only understand where your activity is happening, but also what type of activity it is. Let us say you have comparable-sized networks on Twitter and Facebook, but you're getting more of the results you are looking for on Twitter (*retweets, replies, mentions*) than on Facebook (*comments, likes, shares*) there's something happening on Twitter that's worth investigating.

Investigating each platform you're using and comparing it to others will tell you where your likely prospects or customers are the most engaged. If a clear front-runner emerges, that information will help to inform where your efforts should be concentrated and where you may need to work on growing your audience.

STEP TWO: UNDERSTAND *WHO* IS ENGAGING

Once you know where the conversations are occurring, the next step is to understand who is involved in those conversations. Gaining insight into the individual(s) you are conversing with before you start or join a conversation is critical to your success, because it will influence how you respond. For example, the interactions you have with customers will be very different from those you have with prospects, influencers, partners, or any other segment you will deal with on the social web.

The Interaction Continuum

There are several different perspectives on the types of people interacting with your brand and I developed the *interaction continuum* as a way to categorize people in your audience as well as define how they progress across a prospect's life cycle.

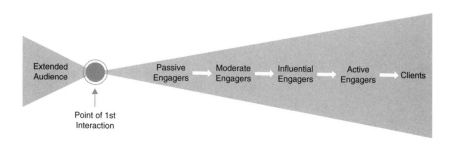

Extended audience: Your extended audience represents the friends of your fans. Think of this as your "above the funnel audience." They will see the activity of someone who "likes" something on your web site, "likes" your page, or updates on your newsfeed and retweets made by your followers, and comments about you sent to their community. These people are most likely to become newly engaged in your content as fans, followers, and friends spread your content to them regularly.

Point of first interaction: The point of first interaction is the point at which someone from your extended audience commits to engaging with your material. This could be as simple as a follow or a like, and it could also be more complex, like a comment or question directly to you.

Passive interactors: In the past, passive interactors have also been called lurkers or listeners. While they have taken the first action, this group typically sits back, silently waiting for the next opportunity to interact. This group is particularly difficult to measure, because they are not taking an active role in interacting with your brand or content, but they are there nonetheless.

Moderate interactors: Moderate interactors engage with your brand or content regularly. This regular interaction is typically in the form of likes, tweets, and retweets or comments. They find value in your content as well as the interaction they get from your brand.

Active interactors: Active interactors are your most passionate and vocal engagers. They participate frequently and in many ways are leaders of the community. They may express issues and concerns with your content, but they are generally your most loyal followers.

Influential interactors: Influential interactors are those that are both active in your brand and are influencing others to join in the conversation as well. They either directly recommend that people track and follow what you are doing or their activity inspires their large base of followers to engage.

Clients: Clients are those that have gone through all the levels of interaction and have purchased your product or service.

Profiling Your Social Audience

Social profiles are the window to your audience. A social profile is an overview of a specific individual across all social networks and contains all available user data and activity history. It provides the background necessary to understanding those you are, or will be, communicating with.

Building social profiles of your audience can be complicated. The challenge is that each network offers different types and varying depths of information on each user. On Facebook, for example, profiles are very robust, but are limited by the privacy settings of the user. Twitter profiles are less robust and require more digging.

More and more automation are being developed to make the collection of social profiles easier. Before we get into some of the advanced methods available, let's start simply. Here are some of the most common ways to get more details on your user:

- **The social network profile:** Start off by investigating the profile of the individual on the social network you are communicating on. For example, if you receive a comment to a Facebook post, look up the individual's Facebook profile. Investigate things such as other brands and fan pages that the user "likes," recent wall posts and interactions, recent tweets and conversations, comments on other blogs, and common relationships or mutual friends. This will give you a better sense of who he or she is and what the context of the conversation is. It will also allow you to personalize a response.

Remember that story I shared from Delta Airlines in the first chapter? That is an excellent example of a brand researching a member of its audience to personalize a response. In that case Rachael specifically mentioned my son as the reason for me wanting to get home early after learning through my Facebook page I was a dad.

▬

- **Other social networks:** Investigate other social networks outside of where the conversation is occurring. Most social networkers maintain multiple profiles, and finding details on them can be easy, assuming you know where to look. If a comment comes in through Twitter, spend a moment to research the background of the individual on Facebook, LinkedIn, Google+, or YouTube. This will provide a much more complete picture of the individual.

- **Klout (www.klout.com):** An excellent resource to understand who is engaging with you, and the best news for you is that it's free. Klout provides detailed scores and analysis on individuals engaging on social media. It identifies the type of personalities they are as well as identifying topics they are influential about and whom they influence. Klout profiles are based primarily on Twitter, but it also includes other networks: Facebook, LinkedIn, Foursquare, YouTube, Instagram, Flickr, Tumblr, and the list is growing.

  Let's assume for a minute that your brand is interested in engaging with me on a social network, but you want to get a better understanding of who I am before you interact. You would go to Klout and enter my Twitter name, @bostonmike.

  From that page you would get a quick snapshot of (1) the person's influence score as determined by Klout, (2) topics the

individual is influential about, and (3) people the user influences. You could also drill into these areas to get additional details.

The challenge brands have with tools like Klout is that their influence score is based on a proprietary algorithm they use to define influence. The challenge is what makes someone influential to one company or industry does not necessarily translate to other brands and industries. As a result, platforms like the Social Marketing Hub allow brands to collect profiles and score the profiles based on an algorithm they define easily within the software. This allows companies to define and identify influencers based on criteria defined by them.

For detailed tips on using **Klout**, check out the Social Fresh Post on Klout.

- **Google search**: This is the old standby. If you are looking to get more details on someone you are engaging with, simply go to Google and search his or her name or Twitter handle. You will find detailed information on who he or she is, which will influence your future interactions.

At this point you are probably thinking: *How do you match all this together with a customer or prospect record in our CRM system?* All these data and information are excellent as is, but it adds much more value when you can match it up with data in your CRM system to get a complete view of the individual.

Pulling and managing a dynamic social profile requires identifying individuals on the social web and tracking their activity up to the point that they engage with your brand. To receive the most benefits from this research, make sure you have people who understand social web tracking to handle these responsibilities. Some of the free tools will help, but they only provide a "moment in time" snapshot. To get deeper insights it's important to collect as many data on the individual as possible.

Some social marketing systems are starting to collect profile data and sync it with CRM systems such as Salesforce.com. The key to implementing a system like this is a unique identifier across the channels, or some piece of information that allows you to tie social profiles together. This unique identifier is typically an e-mail address. E-mail is still the main data point we use to create and set up accounts on social media, and users typically have one e-mail they use for all social networks. Once you gather the e-mail address for an individual it becomes much easier to match who an individual is with their interactions across channels.

A new software space that has emerged facilitates the collection of profiles and is commonly referred to as Social CRM. There are more and more vendors popping up in this space daily. The technology research company Gartner estimates this will be a billion dollar industry by 2013.[1]

Before you invest in software to help build social profiles, here are some tips to help drive prospective conversions and acquisition of e-mail addresses. More details on this will follow in the next chapter:

- Encourage sign-ups as actions ("sign-up for our newsletter," "enter our contest," etc.)
- Drive traffic to your landing pages, blogs, or website that you control
- Facebook opt-ins (pages, etc.)
- Be explicit about privacy

Segmenting Your Social Audience

Once you have a better idea of an individual, bucket the types of interaction you can expect and be sure to segment the audience to better understand how you will respond:

- **Customers:** Is the comment coming from a customer? How valuable is that customer?

- **Influencers:** Is he or she someone generally influential on social media? Is he or she influential in your space? Does he have a track record in being an influencer with other brands?

- **Partners:** Is this coming from a partner of your business?

- **Prospects:** Are they potential prospects for your company?

- **General audience:** Are they part of the general audience?

Paying attention leads to tons of data. The resulting collection of actions, interactions, and content can be prioritized to determine how and with whom you will interact.

Prioritizing how, when, and what you respond to and whom you interact with is the end goal. You will begin to identify specific segments of your audience and prioritize how you want to respond. It's important to reiterate that this engagement could be taking place with individuals who are engaging directly with the content you publish (comments on a blog post) or engaging with conversations that were not initiated by your brand. In the latter case, the individual you are communicating with may not know who you are or what your brand is. Over time, awareness of who you are and what you have to offer will rise.

STEP THREE: DETERMINE *WHAT* AND *WHY*

Now that you understand "who" is interacting, it's time to investigate the "what" and "why" parts of the engagement question. You'll develop a sense of the interactions your audience is making with you, and you can begin to answer the question of how to reinforce the relationship that is developing.

Start by looking at what is being communicated by your audience.

- **Type of interaction:** Is this a service-related request? Is this a potential sales target? Is this a general comment?

- **What is the sentiment of the interaction?** Is it positive or negative?

- **Timing of interactions:** Is this just a one-time interaction or a trend?

Depending on your business focus, you may choose not to interact with every conversation that occurs, even those in which you initiate the dialog. Take Coke for example.

Coke asked their fans a very simple question: "Which song lyric best describes drinking a Coke?" They received over 3,000 comments and 2,000 likes, which can be overwhelming for any brand, even a brand the size of Coke. Their approach is to let their fans control and own the conversation that the company starts. Instead of responding to every single response, they choose to let the audience participate on their own. The initiators at Coke sit back and let them control the conversation around their brand.

Coca-Cola has a very robust and engaging social media strategy. Interested in learning more? Head over to the blog and search for Coca-Cola.

Most of us are operating and engaging with a much smaller audience than Coke, which makes engagement management and strategy much easier. That said, the most important takeaway from the Coke example is that it's not always necessary to respond to each and every comment a brand receives.

While understanding the "what" of individual conversation is important, it's equally important to investigate the broader conversations to identify trends. Here's how to start:

- Choose a large date range, for example the last six months, and compare that data to the preceding six months.

- Compare month to month, especially if your program is relatively new and you don't have many months of data.

- Look at specific pieces of content, and identify the ones that are creating the most engagement.

- On a daily or weekly basis, determine whether there are specific times when your audience is more engaged, whether it's a particular day of the week or a time of day.

This allows you to see trends in active users—how many of your fans visit monthly, weekly, or daily, and what they're doing when they visit.

It also allows you to see trends in interactions—how often and when you are creating buzz in your user community, how many comments and likes do you get on average, what content has generated the most feedback, etc.

You'll begin to see clear spikes in interactions where your content is really successful.

- Compare those spikes in interactions to the piece of content you posted that generated that feedback, and use that information to inform future posts.

- Think about your active base, how much real engagement you're triggering as opposed to just being viewed by your audience. In the case of Facebook, a high number of page views compared to a low number of actual interactions means that you have a small active base and room for improvement.

STEP FOUR: HOW TO INTERACT

With all your data in place, it's time to converse with your audience. Having a plan in place on how to handle engagement with all types of users, who is responsible for engagement, and how it is structured is very important to your overall strategy. More detail on this is provided in Chapter 9, Stand Out Management, but for now start with this simple overview of the things you should be considering.

Who Should Be Involved

Anyone, from the CEO to an intern, can potentially be involved in your engagement strategy. However, there are three common places to recruit talent for a social media team:

1. **The marketing department:** This is the obvious first stop for social media. If your company has an in-house marketing staff, they should already be abreast of the latest social media trends and be given the resources to execute sound strategies for engaging with consumers and creating quality content.

2. **The call center:** If your company already has a team that handles customer complaints and questions, they should continue to perform this duty, but with additional social media training. They should be encouraged to help the company develop new ways of serving customers, using social media. For example, your call-center team may be motivated to participate by posting useful information, allowing customers to help each other solve their problems—which actually decreases call-center workload.

3. **An outside public relations firm or agency:** Companies big and small often bring in additional help to gain expertise and access to relationships their company does not currently have.

Appointing a Team Captain

Once you've built your team, you should pick a team "captain." Industry experts agree that most social media initiatives should have a single manager, who acts as the gatekeeper for all social media communication, though he or she may have other duties within your company. He or she may manage multiple team members who collectively execute your social media strategy. However, this primary point of contact is ultimately responsible for identifying commentary to engage with, routing the correspondence to the necessary party, or responding to all things that can affect brand perception.

The task of selecting an owner for this piece of your strategy is typically a difficult one. A lot of companies appoint the person who is most familiar with social media. It's a natural inclination to select the person who has the most connections on Facebook or Twitter or a popular blog. A word of caution before making this decision: While these individuals have a huge wealth of experience in using social media that you should absolutely leverage as part of your strategy, their experience in this way is often from a personal standpoint, not a business standpoint. Interacting on social networks is very straightforward when it's on behalf of an individual, but becomes much more complicated when done on behalf of a brand. There are more things to account for, like routing, tracking, and overall management, that most individual users never consider on their own. Be sure to identify the right person for the job up front, one who is capable of handling this shift in perspective. Here are some questions to asking before appointing a captain:

- Where does social media fall within the company? Are they a marketing function? Customer service?

- Has an executive championed social media adoption within the company? Which department does he or she represent?

- Is there someone in the company experienced in running social media for a business or brand?

There may also be more than one team manager in each company: for example, one for each brand, industry, or geographic location, if your company manages multiple fronts. The popular site Yelp.com uses this model to great effect, retaining a community manager in each city, who monitors and responds to the ongoing conversation around its brand, engages with users on message boards when appropriate, and promotes events using messaging and newsletter features. The effect is that both the website and the real-time events it organizes are always buzzing with engaged users.

You may also have some initial issues to consider besides your basic task list. These issues might include:

- **Establishing a company voice:** The *Wall Street Journal* and *Rolling Stone* both report on politics, but they do so quite differently. What does your team want to sound like? Once your collective voice is established, how will your team leader maintain consistency between multiple writers? Discuss this with your team.

- **Creating levels of permissions for different users and departments:** If you are using sensitive company information, it may be necessary to create different levels of permissions for your team. For example, your social media strategy may require the help of outside freelancers, who should not see company data or have the ability to respond to comments. Or you may use interns who should not have administrative abilities. Many social media software programs allow for different user settings to solve these issues.

- **Establishing a company social media policy:** Where does your social media strategy begin and end? How much social media use on company time is appropriate? Is your team familiar with the social media norms of each network and how they differ? Do they know who's responsible for responding to a comment, a question directed at a top stakeholder, or an irate customer? Developing a policy for your team that addresses these issues is imperative.

- **Discussing troubleshooting strategies for worst-case scenarios:** This relates to the above. Many marketers fear social media, because it is more difficult to predict and control than traditional media. How will your team handle worst-case scenarios, such as customers who post negative or profane content on your site, security breaches, errors in your content, budget cuts, or sudden turnover within your creative team? Make sure that your team knows the answers to these questions before the first post goes live.

- **Balancing social media duties with other duties within the company:** Unless you have a company with dedicated social media staff, it's likely that your employees have other things to do besides create social media content. Discussing the role it will play in their daily triage of tasks will help each employee to get the job done well.

Defining a Workflow

As you pay attention and identify interaction points across channels you will quickly realize that different departments or individuals need to take ownership of follow-up actions. For example, people expressing customer-service issues should be engaged by service, just as a salesperson should engage people looking for product sales information. Having this prioritization and responsibility map in place is important, as it allows you to both route conversations to the appropriate individual and hold those individuals accountable for follow-up.

This process will likely be tracked manually at the start and will require the process owner reviewing conversations and directing the appropriate parties to engage. While this a good place to begin, it will quickly grow overwhelming. I guarantee it. As your engagement grows, there are multiple systems available today that will help with this process and formalize the routing criteria for your company. Most of these systems fall into the Social CRM or Social Media Management System categories.

Testing

Once your team has settled on a suitable task list and workflow process, it is recommended that you create several pieces of test-content using your new system. Place test pieces in mock-ups, as they will appear to users, and critique them with your company stakeholders and social media team. Not only does this ensure that you'll find and mend the leaks in the system before going live, but it will also help you to create a content stable to pull from in the future, when news may be slow. For this reason, you should choose topics that will always be relevant to users. News editors call this "evergreen content." Examples of evergreen content might be lists of tips or resources, engaging interviews, or profiles that are of interest to your users.

As you test your content your team should consider these questions:

- Does our workflow allow plenty of time for each person to do his or her best work?

- Is every person comfortable with his or her assigned role in the process?

- Does our content have a unified tone and voice that is engaging and in line with the company brand?

- Can we consistently create content with the same quality and tone?

- Are we creating content that we, or our friends, would like to read and share?

Prioritizing Interactions

Not all interactions are created equal. Your audience is a collection of many different types of people with different opinions and objectives, each one driving his or her interest and interactions with your brand in a unique way. These contextual indicators of their intent will allow you to prioritize the engagement and understand the level of urgency to place on possible leads.

The Interaction Grid

An interaction grid defines how you prioritize your follow-up on social channels. It defines who engaged, the specific action, the content, the type of interaction, the priority, and the ownership for follow-up.

Table 4.1 **Sample Interaction Grid**

Who	Action	Content	Type	Priority	Ownership
Brian Zanghi	Comment on blog post	Great post!	Marketing	Low	Sal Giliberto, Marketing
@dkrcarter	Tweet	Looking for new tool	Sales	High	Lian Harrington, Sales
Melissa DiPietro	Comment on Facebook	Looking at your product	Sales	High	Lian Harrington, Sales
Melissa Lefler	Comment on LinkedIn post	Great idea for new product feature	Product	Low	David Carter, Product
Mike Lewis	Comment on blog post	Having trouble accessing the directory	Service	Medium	Steve Own, Services
Steve Tremblay	Comment on Facebook	System crashed!	Service	High	Steve Own, Services

SUMMARY: THE INTERACTION RULES

Interacting with your audience is the cornerstone of your social media strategy. It defines how you are perceived, and that perception is what influences people to interact with your brand or disengage with you completely. The old saying *perception is reality* certainly rings true in social media circles. Being set up to manage and deal with this reality will drive your success.

As you formalize your overall social media strategy, it's important to understand and establish rules of interaction for your social media team. Building and incorporating these rules into your process and culture will help resolve common social media issues before they arise.

1. **Build a brand persona:** In my experience, marketers are very good at defining the persona of their target buyers. This persona helps to define the overall marketing strategy, as it influences the details of your messaging and communication strategy. Likewise, on social media it is important to define your *brand persona* up front and develop your actions from there. Determine the identity, character, and personality of your brand, based on your target market. Understand the values you wish to convey, as well as the message you want to get across.

2. **Join the *right* conversations:** Paying attention lays the groundwork for identifying the right conversations to participate in. That said, how you inject yourself into those conversations is both an art and a science. It's important to understand both the conversation you want to be part of and how to effectively join those conversations.

   You have heard over and over again that "content is king." In social media that's only somewhat true. The truth is that the *context* of your content and engagement is just as, if not more, important on social media outlets. As you engage and interact, your conversations need to be contextually relevant. Entering relevant conversations is critical to the success of your overall program.

3. **Don't be annoying:** There is a fine line between being responsive or proactive and just being downright annoying. Being proactive for the sake of it will make you and your brand appear overbearing. Be sure to calculate how and when you respond, so you don't look annoying.

4. **DON'T JUST SELL!** No one joins a social network with the expressed goal of being sold to. On social media, sales is about making and developing relationships. Start and participate in conversations, don't just jump in with your guns blazing, asking everyone to buy.

5. **Have a process and a captain:** Your team captain can make or break your social strategy. Be sure to make a thoughtful decision and put the right person in place from the start.

6. **Build policies and a code of conduct:** We will talk about policies more in later chapters. For now, just make 100 percent sure that everyone is on the same page regarding how they are expected to interact. You need your frontline social employees on the same page as they interact on the social web.

7. **Capture data and learn from each interaction:** Learn from each engagement and provide a path within the company to adapt and improve products and services over time.

ACTIONS AND TAKEAWAYS

- Identify two or three key influencers in your space, and begin corresponding with them.

- Begin to implement a process where different departments and individuals have ownership over responding to relevant requests.

- Begin to recognize and engage with individuals who have displayed buying intent.

- Document a formal engagement strategy and place ownership on different groups to respond.

- Begin to build a database of social profiles, so you can start to track engagement and leads across the social web.

CHAPTER 5

The Science of Stand Out Interactions

Brian Solis, principal analyst at Altimeter Group and author of the book *Engage,* defines engagement as "the interaction between a consumer or stakeholder and an organization. It is measured . . . as the takeaway value, sentiment and actions that follow the exchange."[1]

These interactions are the enduring effect of content to motivate an audience to do something—the "actions, reactions, and transactions you can shape and steer," according to Solis. "This is why we are no longer merely engaging with an audience, but instead, a sophisticated and connected audience with an audience of audiences."[2]

Whether by instinct or insight, most social marketing practitioners have a good idea of when and where to post content in order to generate the most interaction. There are literally hundreds of theories on how to optimize this, but most are just that: *theories*.

With the data now available for marketers, there is no need for guesswork. Social-marketing programs are increasingly scrutinized by the same data-driven business standards as other marketing programs. Marketers need to know which publishing variables drive meaningful engagement. They should be able to answer:

- What day of the week has the highest post volume?

- What day of the week has the highest interaction rate?

- What day of the week has the highest number of interactions per post?

My job affords me a unique ability to look at interaction data spread across hundreds of companies to see what works and what doesn't. Instead of discussing theories, I want to present data in order to understand the facts about what works and what doesn't in terms of stimulating interaction within your audience. I want to answer some related questions and take a scientific approach to verify the current best practices and to find patterns in data that encourage the development of new best practices. To accomplish this, I will present and discuss the aggregate data collected across all Awareness clients.

I analyzed over 200,000 posts to Facebook, Twitter, YouTube, Slideshare, Flickr, and Wordpress published over the course of 2011. Posts are defined as status updates, blog posts, tweets, and video, photo, or document uploads. In addition, I investigated the 31 million and more interactions on those posts. Interactions are defined as comments, likes, shares, @ replies, and retweets.

Before we look at the numbers in more detail, it's important to let you know a little more about the data I am working with:

- Data span 100 randomly selected Awareness customers
- Awareness customers range from large, multibillion-dollar international companies to small, privately held companies.
- Industries include an even split between B2B and B2C

WHEN TO POST?

A common question posed by social media practitioners is "when is the best time of day to post content to social channels in order to maximize the likelihood of interactions?" To answer this question, let's start by looking at the total number of posts per day.

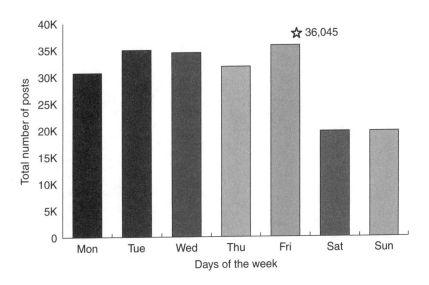

Not surprisingly, 81 percent of all posts occur on weekdays. Friday has the distinction of being the day with highest volume of posted messages, at 36,045, while Sunday has the lowest number of posts, at 19,868.

These findings are not necessarily an indication that Fridays are the most productive day to post content in order to generate interactions, nor does it suggest that Sundays are the least productive. They do, however, indicate the publishing habits in the market, and alternatively suggest certain days when too much content is being published, possibly making it more difficult for your message to be seen.

Let's investigate that same group of posts and look at the *Interaction Rate*. The interaction rate is the total number of interactions by day of the week. The following graph shows the total number of interactions per day across all channels.

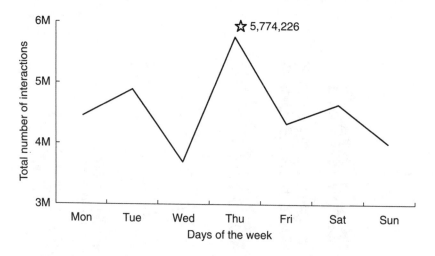

It was somewhat surprising to see a spike in interactions on Thursday, with 50 percent more interactions than on Fridays, even though about 15 percent more posts were published on Fridays than on Thursdays. It's also worth noting that Wednesday pro-

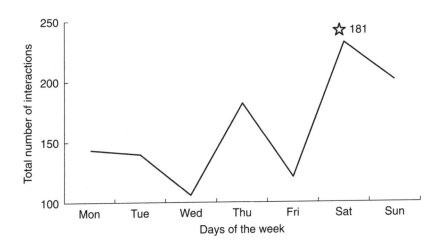

duced the lowest number of interactions by far, despite being one of the highest posting-volume days.

This finding may be a useful benchmark for weekday interactions, but the data also revealed an opportunity worth exploring: Even though the number of posts was lowest on weekends, the interaction rate was over 200 percent higher than on Wednesday, the lowest day for interactions during the week. The reduced number of brand posts on weekends, coupled with the higher engagement rate, indicates an opportunity to experiment with weekend posts to see how it affects interaction rates. Brands often struggle to post over the weekend or during off-hours, an obstacle that can be overcome by using software that allows users to schedule posts in a queue.

Tactical tip: Thursday is the best day of the week to post content to stimulate interactions. Do not ignore posting on weekends.

TIME OF DAY

What time of day is best to post content in order to maximize interactions? Looking at the volume of posts by hour and by day answers this question.

The majority of posts originated between 11 a.m. and 5 p.m. Eastern time, with a peak over the lunch hour, from 12 noon to 2 p.m. Eastern time. There is a moderate spike in the early morning hours on Monday and Friday. The highest-volume time for posting was between 12 noon and 2 p.m. Eastern time on Fridays.

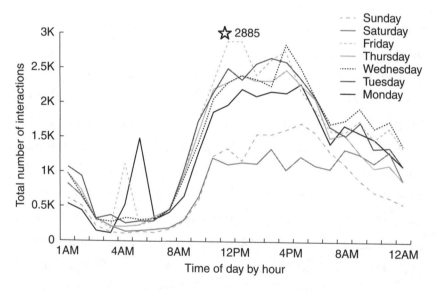

Similarly, when looking at interactions by hour, we find an obvious peak between 12 noon and 2 p.m. Eastern time, with the highest volume of interactions during the 2 p.m. hour.

In terms of the best time of day to post, there does appear to be a correlation between number of posts in a given period and interactions on those posts. Based on these findings, marketers should consider experimenting to see what time of day generates the most

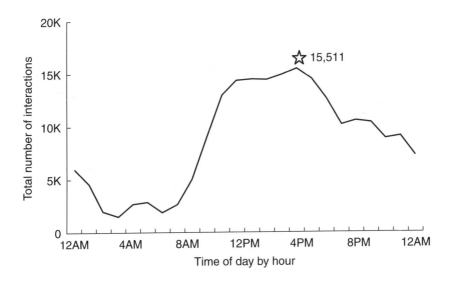

interaction with their particular audience. One way to do this is to compare the engagement results from two Facebook posts, each targeting a similar dominant marketing area, at different times, with the same message.

Tactical tip: The best time of the day to post in order to maximize interactions is between 1 p.m. and 4 p.m. Eastern time. Experiment with posting at different times of the day to see what works for your specific audience and brand.

POST HALF-LIFE: MEASURING INTERACTION OVER TIME

Which channel is best for generating engagement? I like to think about this question in terms of efficient use of content: *How long will a piece of content be in play?*

Analyzing the millions of comments collected in the system allows us to understand the life span of posts, or the "post half-life," by channel. I tracked the number of comments hourly for ten days after the content was published. This study does not consider time of day, sentiment, or content quality.

Fundamental differences in the design of social media channels affect post half-life. For instance, content posted to Twitter and Facebook had a very short life span, with 99 percent of engagement occurring in the first ten days. This is because Facebook and Twitter use a news-stream format, which pushes content away from the viewer's attention very quickly. Posts to these platforms earn the majority of engagement in the first hour.

On Flickr, YouTube, and Wordpress, where engagement generally depends on visitors actively coming to the sites, via search engine traffic for example, the engagement patterns are quite different. Content on Flickr earned 82 percent of its engagement during the first ten days. YouTube and WordPress content earned 34 percent of engagement during the first ten days.

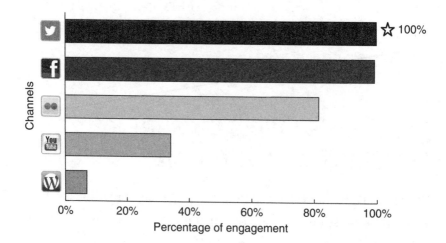

- **Twitter and Facebook:** Not surprisingly, the content half-life of Twitter and Facebook was very short; 99 percent of engagement occurred within the first ten days on both channels (99.8 percent for Twitter; 99.8 percent and 99.3 percent for Facebook). Engagement had been completely exhausted by the tenth day.

- **Flickr:** Content on Flickr saw 82 percent of its engagement realized during the first ten days.

- **YouTube:** Content here received 34 percent of engagement during the first ten days.

- **WordPress:** Content here received 34 percent of all engagement during the first ten days.

These data follow an expected pattern. Facebook and Twitter have news-stream formats that push content away from the viewer attention very quickly. In fact, the first hour after publishing a post represents the majority of the engagement in those platforms. A post's half-life on Flickr, YouTube, and WordPress, on the other hand, generally depends on the visitors to the site, search engine traffic, or percentage of engagement.

PROFILING THE ENGAGEMENT

Ten days is a very long time for content presented in a news-stream format. In fact, if we review the engagement by the first few hours, we can see an even more dramatic difference. Below I have profiled each social network across the first 24 hours.

The following chart shows aggregate comments over the first 24-hour period.

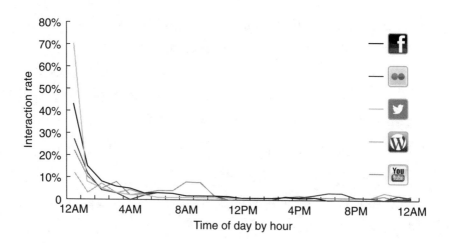

When we viewed engagement patterns across the first 24 hours on these channels, the differences became more pronounced. Interestingly, YouTube continued to generate significant instances of engagement for almost ten hours. YouTube, Flickr, and WordPress all experienced upticks for the first 24 hours. Facebook and Twitter, however, dropped dramatically in the first hour after publication.

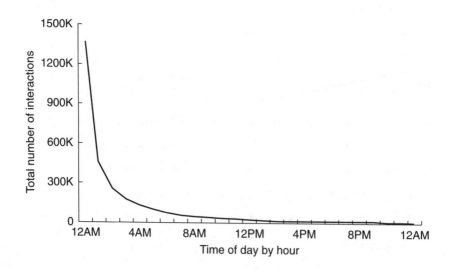

UNDERSTANDING THE RESULTS

In the analysis, content on Twitter dropped off dramatically in the first hour; within three hours it had reached 90 percent of its potential interaction. Similarly, Facebook also stimulated immediate interaction, but it stretched out over a slightly longer period. After 12 hours, Facebook content had seen 90 percent of its potential interaction.

The other three channels, Flickr, WordPress, and YouTube, generate a lot of interaction soon after publishing, but continued to generate comments for a relatively long time. I believe this is because content from these channels is very discoverable by search engines. In the case of YouTube, the viral nature of the video can create interaction blooms at unanticipated moments in the life of the content piece.

Here are some tactical tips based on the findings:

- **Twitter:** Include hashtags in your posts, so a current content item can create curiosity about past posts. For example, "How to fix a leak #homerepair." This may draw previous tweets back into view if the user searches #homerepair. Hashtags are also an important measure of engagement, as you can see the relevance of your content over time. Finally, hashtags allow you to capture engagements where users may not have mentioned you by name but have shared your content.

- **Facebook:** Publish to Facebook at least daily. Content in Facebook shows the engagement as part of the content (that is, you can see the number of likes and actual comments inline), and lots of engagement bring it into a top story. Write the content that is proven to engage fans—phrase your content as a question or ask for an opinion. Facebook's new feature, "Timeline," may have a dramatic impact on these results. This new feature encourages viewers to explore historic content and may change the dynamics completely.

- Cross-publish rich content to Flickr, WordPress, and YouTube to expose search engines to your content. Use those pages to promote all your social media channels. Include "Tweet this" and links to Facebook Fan pages.

Now that you have a better idea of when to publish, let's investigate strategies that will help you stimulate interactions with your audience.

ACTIONS AND TAKEAWAYS

- Experiment publishing on different days of the week, and track how much interaction is generated for each post.
- Experiment with posting on the weekends.
- Publishing toward the end of the workday is best, but continue to experiment to see what works for you.
- Build and drive traffic toward landing pages to maximize overall exposure.

CHAPTER 6

Stand Out Approaches to Stimulating Interaction

Facilitating interactions with your audience can be tricky. The objective is to inspire your audience to interact with the content and information you provide, and to do so in ways that draw in more viewers. It's both an art and a science, and when done correctly, it will help distinguish your social marketing strategy.

Have you ever found yourself at a crowded party, stuck in a boring conversation with someone who seems to talk only about himself? You instinctively begin to tune him out and try to find a way to excuse yourself from the conversation in order to focus on other things.

On the flip side, you might notice that a good conversation at the same party is more like an easy volley between tennis players, with appropriate questions and useful, thoughtful, honest answers moving back and forth in a timely fashion. When both sides are interacting in this way, everyone has a good time and raves about the party.

Generating that same feeling of enjoyable engagement should be your goal, so it is important to keep this in mind when crafting your social media plan. Do you want to increase sales? Create a stronger brand identity and awareness? Get more sign-ups for your e-newsletter? Having specific goals will help you focus your approach and ensure that your conversation will be well received by those participating online.

Interacting with users in this way can provide multiple benefits. For example:

- It can inspire conversations about your brand.
- You can learn more about your customers.
- You can increase competitive intelligence.

To reap these benefits, you must be prepared to engage your audience with a number of different entertaining tactics that benefit your customers.

STRATEGIES FOR INCREASING INTERACTION

Armed with the data you know about the timing and frequency of postings, we're ready to move on to the strategies and tactics to maximize engagement with your audience.

1. ASK QUESTIONS

The strategy: Engage your users with relevant questions, in the form of Twitter or Facebook posts, polls, and other opinion trackers.

Best practices: Don't worry about asking questions that specifically pertain to your business, but rather, ask questions that people on your site would be interested in answering. You can use keyword trackers to determine the questions that your customers are already asking or answering around a certain subject. Questions can be posed to users via Twitter or Facebook, or in the form of polls, surveys, and quizzes. The more questions you ask, the more interactions you'll get—and if your business can sustain posing a daily question, you'll have users coming back to check for new questions and answers on a regular basis.

Examples: Major Legue Baseball (MLB) asks its fan base a lot of questions on a daily basis. Questions generally center on the most controversial baseball games and issues of the day, usually around a big game or rivalry about which fans have strong opinions. This helps facilitate simple and entertaining interactions among the league's most passionate fans.

Why these work: Questions make it easy to interact, and they make it clear that the business—and their readers—is interested in hearing the answers. This type of interaction acts as a motivator for content developers, ensuring that questions and answers are relevant, interesting, and if possible, useful to their readers.

2. OFFER A DEAL OR PROMOTION

The strategy: Generate engagement by giving things away. According to several studies, the number one reason why most people follow brands is to receive specials and promotions.

Interested in learning what makes people want to follow a brand? Head over to the blog and check out this great infographic from *Get Satisfaction*.

Best practices: Consistently offer small deals to build your readership base and get them coming back to your site. You don't need to give away your own product—any product that is attractive to your desired audience will achieve your goal of engagement. Partner with other companies to package smaller deals together for added value and cross-promotion. Consider inviting your users to follow, friend, or become a fan of your social-networking site in order to become eligible for deals, to submit their e-mail addresses for follow-up, or simply to leave comments on your blog to increase engagement.

Example: Mars Random Acts of Chocolate

From *"Mars Distributing Random Acts of Chocolate"*: Mars Chocolate North America coordinated 50,000 Mars Random Acts of Chocolate on September 6, 2011, by delivering free samples of its iconic chocolate brands to New Yorkers via bike messengers in Manhattan. Mars Random Acts of Chocolate was developed to distribute nine million of the company's chocolate products to fans across the United States this fall.

Americans were also able to score free M&M's, Snickers, TWIX, 3 Musketeers, or Milky Way brand chocolates a number of other ways, including logging on to either the M&M's, Snickers, TWIX, 3 Musketeers, or Milky Way Facebook pages on September 8, 2011, to secure a free coupon of their choice, as well as the opportunity to give a free coupon to one of their Facebook friends (while supplies lasted).

"We all know that chocolate can instantly brighten someone's day," said Debra A. Sandler, Chief Consumer Officer, Mars Chocolate North America. "We plan to do our part to brighten moods in America by distributing more than nine million free chocolate bars, but we also encourage our fans to show how thoughtful they are by doing a Mars Random Acts of Chocolate for someone they care about."[1]

Why these work: Deals like these get users to visit your site more frequently, spend more time on the site, give feedback on the products you're promoting, share your deals with their friends, and if the deal involves an experience, bring their friends along when they visit your business to use the deal.

3. HOLD A CONTEST

The strategy: Stimulate competition and give something away on a larger scale.

Best practices: Start with a goal—for example, gaining more fans and followers, improving brand visibility or identity, or driving more traffic to your site. Then look for ways to use cross-promotion to up the visibility and the participation in your contest. When planning your contest, keep in mind that the spoils do not have to go to the users themselves; often social media campaigns center around asking users to vote for a cause or an organization who will win much-needed dollars or resources.

Example: *USA Today*'s #America Wants Twitter Campaign (An excerpt from *ThoughtPick*, published in May 2010).

The #AmericaWants hashtag contest was conceived by Social Media strategist Alex Nicholson as part of *USA Today*'s larger "What America Wants" brand campaign, designed to illustrate *USA Today*'s connection with the American experience and readers' engagement with the brand on multiple media platforms.

The charity that had the most retweets of the message "#AmericaWants [charity name] to get a full-page ad in USA TODAY" with its name in the tweet between Tuesday, April 13, and Friday, April 16, was declared the victor.

Buzz generated: All in all, users posted more than 60,000 tweets in support of more than 500 organizations. The tweets reached an estimated 67 million users on Twitter.[2]

#AmericaWants @PETA to get a full-page ad in **USA TODAY** to help stop the Canadian seal slaughter: www.canadasshame.com/ Pls RT!

malleryknox - Twitter - 2 hours ago

Could win $189K free ad for clean water if you RT: #AmericaWants @charitywater to get a full-page ad in **USA TODAY**. Please RT

rafaelofaria - Twitter - 4 hours ago

I am so happy that millions of people will be introduced to @TWLOHA because #AmericaWants them to have a (free) ad in **USA Today**. Congrats!

kellykins_256 - Twitter - 4 hours ago

RT @MDAnews: Congrats to @TWLOHA on winning **USA Today's** #AmericaWants full-page ad. Thanks again to everyone who tweeted to support @MDA ...

Kim_Bruna - Twitter - 4 hours ago

#AmericaWants @MakeAWish to get a full-page ad in **USA TODAY**. Please RT!

robin60179 - Twitter - 5 hours ago

RT @sargeknives: I second that! RT @glennrsmith #AmericaWants the Boy Scouts of America to get a full-page ad in **USA TODAY**.

pack415 - Twitter - 5 hours ago

#AmericaWants @TrevorProject to get a full-page ad in **USA TODAY**.

Why these work: By asking users to tweet about their favorite charities, *USA Today* drew new users to their Twitter feed and became associated with the good causes they sought to promote, while their followers' favorite charities also enjoyed a boost in publicity due to *USA Today*'s visibility in the media. (For the record, To Write Love on Her

Arms, a charity combating depression and suicide, gar-
nered the highest number of votes.)

Meanwhile, Southwest Airlines—whose Facebook fan page
has over 2.1 million fans and counting—frequently offers
deals and contest eligibility to "fans only," leading savvy
travelers to follow them for deals.

Both campaigns increased engagement, grew the companies'
social media audience, and spread a message that was consistent with (or improved upon) the brands' identities.

TWO STAND OUT CONTESTS

Let's have some fun and demonstrate a couple of contest in action!

Stand Out Facebook Contest!

For 12 months, starting in November 2012, when this book is published, I will give a $50 Amazon.com gift card to one reader every
month who "Likes" the Stand Out Social Marketing Facebook Page
(www.facebook.com/standoutsocial). The gift card recipient will be
randomly selected from all new users from the previous month and
will be awarded on the first day of the following month. Winners will
be announced on the Facebook page starting on December 1, 2012,
continuing through November 1, 2013.

#StandOut Twitter Challenge!

Again, for 12 months starting in November 2012, when this book
is published, I will give a $25 Amazon.com gift card every month
to one randomly selected reader who tweets a pictures of him- or

herself holding a copy of *Stand Out Social Marketing* (be sure to include the hashtag #standout). The gift card recipient will be randomly selected from all tweets from the previous month and will be awarded on the first day of the following month. Winners will be announced on the Stand Out Facebook page starting on December 1, 2012, continuing through November 1, 2013.

4. CREATE A GAME

The strategy: Increase the engagement of a particular customer base, and/or underscore a particular brand message, with a customized online game.

Best practices: Developing games can be very expensive, so be sure to review the costs before embarking on this strategy. Make sure the game developed for your brand communicates your brand message and expresses what you want to say. Choose your target game player carefully (and don't bother designing games for which your audience has no time or aptitude). Consider the difference between a game that will be played solo, completely within the Internet space, and an interactive game that requires users to join teams or go to places in their city.

Example: SCVNGR's game for Swarovski's "Discover Your Light" campaign.

Why it works: The game, which was produced in conjunction with an independent film and the up-and-coming game developer SCVNGR, underscores Swarovski's message of romance, adventure, youth, and sophistication. The crystal

jewelry was portrayed as "treasure" with a treasure hunt that allowed users to try out SCVNGR's service as they roamed the city looking for Swarovski's goods. It increased engagement with both companies and likely generated useful feedback and buzz for both products.

5. HOST A LIVE CHAT

The strategy: Invite users to witness and/or join an actual conversation around a topic related to your brand.

Best practices: Keep content relevant, keep it moving, keep it interesting, and keep it clean. You don't need special software to experiment with the elements of live chat, which can be incorporated into your existing social media that is, inviting people to live-tweet at an event you're already hosting, comment on your Facebook page about a project that's under way, or contribute questions to a conversation happening between two experts in your industry online or via video. This method works especially well for specialized audiences of people who don't normally have the opportunity to converse in real life.

Examples: WWE's Live Chat, #Awarenessinc Webinars.

Why these work: Around each weekly TV show (*RAW* and *Smackdown*) and all live pay-per-view events, WWE.com hosts a chat session that resembles a sports talk show: Moderators banter about the action and select user comments to highlight that help carry the conversation forward. Users are thus encouraged to keep posting, and to post clever commentary in order to make it into the public conversation.

WWE "gets" social marketing and is consistently innovating their approach. Want to learn more? See how WWE stacks up to their competition UFC by heading over to the blog and searching for WWE vs UFC.

Meanwhile, Awareness hosts bi-weekly webinars with social media experts and thought leaders to allow users in the space to learn about new trends and best practices. Interaction is encouraged by inviting audience members to ask questions of the host and presenter via twitter using the hashtag #awarnessinc. Typically, webinars lose audience over time (on average, 20 percent as the session goes on). The Awareness webinar audience, on the other hand, grows, on average by 15 percent, something we associate with the conversation happening on Twitter.

In both cases, users can also visit the site to view past conversations. These examples represent two opposite ends of a spectrum: one, which encompasses passionate, playful conversation around a sport, and the other as a straightforward conversation, with resources offered to serious businesspeople about their industry. Both provide an interesting, dynamic, and honest way of presenting real-time information to the people who want it.

6. USE PHOTOS AND VIDEOS

The strategy: The cliché says that a picture is worth a thousand words, and it's true. You can use images and videos to say something about your company and invite opinions, tagging, and sharing. About 65 percent of people are mainly visual learners,3 meaning that they easily pick up information that engages their ability to see. Visual learners often associate the things they learn with the images they saw when they first learned the material.

Best practices: Photos and videos not only generate higher interactions online, they also have priority when Facebook's Edgerank determines what to include in the Top News feed. More time in the news feed means more consumer engagement.

Example: The Mercedes Facebook page regularly posts multiple pictures, videos, and albums a week. Of the 31 posts made during the month of September 2011, posts containing photos or videos generated an average of 232 percent more Likes, 1,076 percent more Shares, and 303 percent more comments than other posts containing no photos or video. It makes sense that photos and videos generate the highest interaction rate, as they draw the user in visually, are easily digestible, and can elicit an emotional response quickly.

Why this works: Photos and videos make sharing colorful information about a company fun and easy. They also allow users to feel more connected to, and invested in, the companies who distribute this kind of information well. The images immediately draw attention from the observer and inherently encourage interaction.

7. HAVE AN OPINION
(EVEN IF IT'S NOT POPULAR)

The strategy: Drop a controversial opinion into an area where people have strong opinions or loyalties (cities, sports teams, etc.) and invite comments.

Best practices: Be careful with this one! You don't want to be known solely as the business that bashed the beloved local sports team or took an unpopular and unnecessary stance on a controversial political issue. If you're opinionated, you'll surely gain engagement from some, but risk alienating others. The best way to remain above serious reproach is to comment only on issues in which your brand is already an established authority in the space.

Example: Perez Hilton's celebrity slams.

Why these work: Perez Hilton knows his subjects well and spouts unapologetic and controversial opinions in every post. As a result, he has a strong, engaged following. He has also amassed a host of detractors, who also want to participate in the conversation, and their commentary has only cemented Perez Hilton's popularity in the celebrity-gossip world.

8. ENGAGE YOUR MOST PASSIONATE FANS

The strategy: Enable your fan base to promote your brand through social channels.

Best practices: Engage with specific users and they will feel like part of the community. Make sure to keep barriers to entry low—the more the merrier with fan pages, but you lose users with each hoop they need to jump through. For example, instead of making users set up entire profiles just to interact on your site, require minimal input, such as entering a user name or e-mail address.

Example: Major League Baseball launched the MLBlogs program a few years ago. The program allows fans to create free blogs focused generally on baseball or around their favorite teams. MLB partnered with WordPress to develop and implement the concept, which now boasts thousands of contributors.

Why these work: These spaces encourage users to indulge in their obsessions in the company of like-minded individuals. The MLBlogs example enables fans to participate as citizen journalists.

9. CREATE STARS

The strategy: Allow real people to emerge as authorities on a subject related to your company's business.

Best practices: Champion your most vocal users. Engage with your more regular and vocal fans often, and ask for their opinions to help position them as liaisons between your company and the general public. Users trust fellow users more than they do a representative that is on your company's payroll. Once your "stars" have built up their own reputations within your constructed online community, you can even give them more official roles—such as comment moderator or guest poster. Internet stardom is a popular goal among social media users, and your online community could help people get there.

Example: Social Media Examiner's Top Fans, Yelp's Elite Members.

Why these work: The most vocal and enthusiastic users of these sites have become well-known and trusted personalities who help to strengthen the brands and encourage more users to participate. Social media Examiner ranks contributors to identify the most passionate people on their Facebook page and rank them. Yelp's Elite members are often treated to exclusive events—they are the company's inner circle, and many users aspire to be among their ranks. Both scenarios reward users for their continued engagement and create communities with established personalities in which users are more likely to engage with each other, not just the brand.

10. HOST A GUEST POST

The strategy: Find experts or colleagues in the space willing to cross-promote your interests, provide you with interesting new content, and lend credibility to your brand with a guest posting. Leverage their expertise and following to drive traffic to your blog.

Best practices: This works two ways—you can post content on a partner's site or you can enlist a relevant personality to post on *your* site. Newer brands might partner with more established brands or individuals to gain credibility, or older brands might want to partner with individuals or organizations to refresh their brand's relevance. It's also a great way for bloggers to gain more exposure.

Looking for some help finding guest posters? Swing over to the blog and search for **Guest Posts** to direct you to a helpful article from Social Media Today. http://socialmediatoday.com/kwameboame/178154/10-places-find-blogs-guest-post.

Example: Guest posting is very common in the software space, and I decided to use a real example featuring

Awareness. We regularly feature guest bloggers to discuss specific topics and areas of expertise.

Why this works: The guest blogger posts about a subject area of expertise. When the post is live, he or she promotes it and drives traffic to your blog. This can help bring his or her following to your brand page and increase traffic and awareness for your company. Similarly, having an executive featured as a guest blogger on a partner site can help drive traffic and increase awareness.

11. ASK FOR ENGAGEMENT

The strategy: be Bold and ask your audience to engage with you. On Facebook, ask them to comment, like, or share content. On Twitter, ask for responses or retweets. On blogs ask for comments. It's that simple, just ask.

Example: Amazon Movies & TV uses the "please retweet" tag regularly to spread the word on deals.

Why this works: People generally respond to a call to action. Whether you are asking to retweet, comment, post, or like, asking your audience to respond generates the highest likelihood for engagement.

These strategies of interaction are great for those moments when you're perched on the margins of a conversation that is happening in social media or when you're unsure of what to say or how to get users to talk. Tried-and-true strategies like those listed above are sure to give you a good place to start. The choice you make about which tactics to

Amazon Movies & TV

Get $2 towards music @amazonmp3 for a limited time. Find out how and please retweet: amzn.to/nmePTI

29 Sep via Social Manager Publisher

☆ Favorite ℃ Retweet ↰ Reply

Retweeted by bradfordneal and 100+ others

try should center on your company's goals—whether you want to update your brand identity, collect e-mail addresses for your e-newsletter, or get feedback from your customers.

Be forewarned: There's a lot of trial and error involved in finding the perfect strategy for your company. Some strategies will win you scores of fans, but may not an online community make, while others may not be sustainable in terms of cost or time. Do not get discouraged. Most social media strategies work best when they focus on testing one or two tactics at a time. So choose carefully, lest you confuse your users or spread your marketing resources too thinly. It is to be hoped that, as you improve your approach toward interaction and hear more about what your particular users have to say about your brand, you'll develop your own best practices along the way.

ACTIONS AND TAKEAWAYS

- Brainstorm creative topics and activities that your customer base enjoys most.

- Develop questions, discussion points, and resources that can be easily posted to social media outlets and that elicit quick responses.

- Develop longer-term activities, games, or collaborations with partners that can be fed through social media to increase overall engagement with your brand.

CHAPTER 7

Stand Out Content

Content is the single most important aspect of your social-marketing strategy. It allows you to reach the right audience, interact with that audience, and stand out on the social web. Content marketing has grown to become a significant area of focus for every business engaging in social media marketing. Understanding the intricacies of publishing and managing that content is critical to the overall success of your social media program.

IF CONTENT IS KING, CONTEXT IS QUEEN

When we talk about social content, we are talking about a very broad category of social marketing. This includes original content, such as blog posts, video, Facebook Wall posts, Facebook events, Twitter posts, photos, *as well as* your responses to the conversations you are interacting in. Social content is the powerful catalyst for engaging your audience throughout the marketing process—nurturing them from passive interactors to buyers, keeping your brand at the top of prospects' minds when they are ready to buy, and adequately addressing specific mentions (positive or negative) about your brand and products. The quality of your content determines your audience's engagement and your ability to grow your audience over time. The golden rule of effective content is: *Content should be focused on the needs of your prospects and customers—not focused on you, your company, or your product.* This is extremely important to keep in mind, as businesses often lose sight of it when engaging in the social marketplace.

Content comes in different flavors, depending on your goals, industry and size, and the social platform you engage in. Content also differs by type of company. Typically, B2B companies need to focus on industry-specific educational content that helps drive better understanding of the issues and the challenges particular to that industry, while B2C companies need to tie more closely with their customers' lifestyles while balancing special offers.

You have probably heard the expression "content is king;" however, a recent conversation with David Berkowitz, senior director of Emerging Media and Innovation for digital marketing agency 360i, gave a different take:

> Content that works [in social media] is not formulaic—it is a balance between promotions, such as coupons, specials, and new product announcements, and "equity posts," which are

based on the needs of the buyer. The content creation rule of thumb we use: 2:1 in favor of equity posts.[1]

Translation: Content is important, but CONTEXT is really king on social media. In other words, you can produce fantastic, well thought out content, but it will fall on deaf ears if it's delivered out of context. Brands and individuals that continuously "sell" through social channels are often, if not always, ignored.

Christine Major, corporate communications manager at Demandware, talks about how Demandware uses content as part of their marketing mix:

> We can see what's working and what's not. When we publish educational blog posts around hot topics, such as how to build a storefront within your Facebook Fan page, we get significantly more views and comments than traditional product-focused blog posts. Content that offers our collective expertise at Demandware, and helps our prospects and clients with their top questions or challenges, is the way we build trust and lasting connections. Ultimately we want our blog to become a destination for our industry.[2]

Content development is an iterative process, which needs to be informed by a key set of metrics so it can be optimized over time. Measuring what content works within a social platform and repeatedly testing it against industry best practices allows companies to build expertise around content creation and engagement. This knowledge enables them to prioritize social marketing resources for an optimal return on their social media investment.

My company, Awareness, makes sure our content is delivered in context across multiple social channels.

CASE STUDY THE AWARENESS CONTENT
MARKETING MACHINE

The cornerstone of the success of Awareness is the content marketing engine, which pumps thousands of inquiries to the sales engine every month.

As a provider of social marketing software, it makes sense that Awareness spends a significant amount of our marketing budget on content marketing. Every month e-books, white papers, case studies, videos, and webinars are produced to help educate the audience on the benefits and value of social media marketing. This educational and thought leadership material serves to help customers better utilize the software, positions Awareness as a thought leader in the space, and drives customer acquisition.

The key to the marketing engine is content syndication and making sure each piece of content is used in multiple ways. For example, a white paper that is produced is marketed through sponsored e-mail blasts and banner ads, spread through Twitter and

Download whitepapers, ebooks, and chapters from Awareness

Facebook, blogged, and turned into a webinar. On average, each piece of content is used in six or more unique ways.

Here is what's important about the Awareness approach to content:

1. Content is produced with the objective of positioning Awareness as a thought leader, as opposed to simply generating demand.

2. Each piece of content is used in multiple ways.

3. Content is produced to help the audience, not simply to talk about Awareness.

Sal Giliberto, Director of Demand Generation at Awareness, Inc., says "Content is the catalyst that drives our marketing programs. Our philosophy is each piece of content is the core of six to ten additional content pieces that are based on that foundational piece." The focus is always on the customer, not the product. The social media resources and research we deliver is of benefit to a business audience, regardless of if they are or will ever become a client.

SOCIAL OUTPOSTS AND HOME BASE

In September 2008, Chris Brogan introduced the concept of "outposts" and "home base." The idea is that outposts represent "touchpoints away from your main online presence, where you connect with others in some way."[3] Home base is your primary online presence, the place where you direct the traffic from your outposts. Chris summarizes in his blog post:

> Thinking of your primary online presence as your home base, and then thinking of the places where you make social connec-

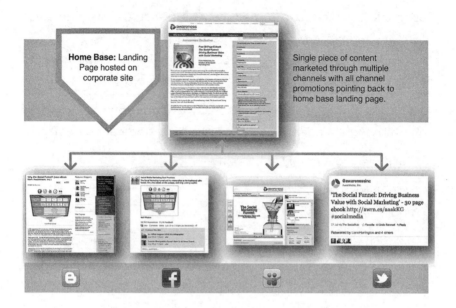

tions as your outposts (I realized I forgot LinkedIn, but I'm there too, obviously), then you see how you might prioritize your time and/or how you might try keeping the value chain alive.[4]

Businesses should structure under the same framework. While you communicate and engage across many outposts, it's important to direct traffic back to your home base. Your home base should be in the form of a blog, landing page, or your corporate website. This is critical because of social search-engine optimization (SEO). Your home base will serve as the collection point for all your activity and will be optimized for SEO. In addition, it serves as a mechanism for conversion events that you can track. Those conversion events are page views, a download, or a sale, and they are much more easily tracked on a destination you control.

AMERICAN CANCER SOCIETY: A MULTI-CHANNEL SOCIAL HUB AND SPOKE MODEL

American Cancer Society (ACS) understands that their social presence serves as outposts to drive traffic to a primary web presence.

I recently connected with Karen Rose, Social Media Strategist for the national home office of the American Cancer Society, in Atlanta, Georgia, to discuss in detail how they use social media to drive thought leadership, awareness, and lead generation.

Besides their national home office, there are 12 regional divisions of ACS, each managing its social marketing independently, each with social media agendas and strategies of its own. The national home office of ACS primarily uses Facebook, with its Fan Page counting close to 250,000 members, and Twitter approaching 200,000 followers. The ACS team actively publishes content, which includes supporting multiple blogs, such as *Dr. Len's Cancer Blog*

authored by Dr. Lichtenfeld (the Deputy Chief Medical Officer for the national office of the ACS), *Expert Voices* authored by experts who discuss timely cancer topics, and the *Choose You* blog, which encourages women to put their own health first.

ACS has embraced the social web as one of their most effective marketing channels—Karen puts it simply: "We really just need to be where the people are." Karen and her team started to track conversations about cancer in the early days of social media. They quickly realized there was a lot of inaccurate information and misconceptions about cancer being published and shared on a daily basis. "Our team had to intervene," Karen says with passion. "We needed to provide sound medical advice and offer ACS's vetted resources to help patients and their loved ones cope with the disease."

"We want to inform people about the many ACS resources we have, so they can stay well and get well," continues Karen. ACS's goal is to inform and educate about screenings, guidelines, support groups, and medical resources. "ACS uses social media as the spokes of our hub to pull people back to our web properties," comments Karen.

The ACS main Facebook Fan page—*American Cancer Society*—focuses on cancer, cancer-related topics, survivorship, and caregiving, and serves primarily as an information and educational resource. Other nationally managed Facebook Fan pages, such as *Making Strides Against Breast Cancer* and *Relay for Life*, are event-based pages. The *Relay for Life* Fan page, backed by over 110,000 passionate followers, exists to support a fun-filled overnight event celebrating survivorship and to raise money for research and programs coordinated by ACS. The ACS *More Birthdays* Facebook page, with over 300,000 fans, was created to celebrate birthdays and sur-

vivorship. The *Choose You* Fan page is directed toward women who want to have their own conversation about cancer prevention.

MULTI-CHANNEL PUBLISHING BY THE NUMBERS

As part of writing this book, I began a study to document the extent businesses of all sizes are adopting multi-platform social media strategies, assessing satisfaction with this diversified communications approach, and recording best practices and metrics that are emerging from their early experiences.

The first stage of the research consisted of two parts: an online survey that was posted in January and promoted through a variety of social media channels. The survey received 512 responses, of which 325 came from small businesses and 187 from companies with more than 1,000 employees.

The companies surveyed were using an average of eight social networks to distribute content and engage with their audiences. It should come as no surprise that, of the platforms in use, the most popular are Facebook, Twitter, and blogs, with LinkedIn in fourth place.

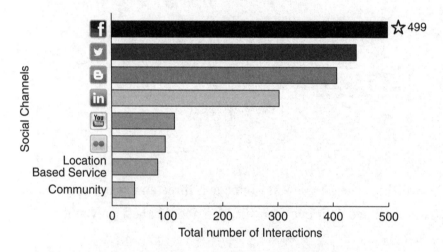

Wikipedia lists over 200 social networking sites on their lists, and it seems like new social networks are popping up daily. This increasing popularity of social networks has marketers scrambling to understand which to engage with in order to reach their audiences.

This research provides some answers but also leads to a bigger question: How many social networks should your brand be participating in? This is a BIG question and, unfortunately, there is no simple answer, because each channel takes time, money, and focus to participate in effectively.

Andrew Patterson, manager of new media at MLB advanced media says "the decision on [the right] number of social media channels for a company is contextual. What is important is how consistent you are with engaging in a social media channel. You can't be there one day and gone the next. If you have the resources to be consistent across multiple channels, then by all means do it. But if you spread yourself too thin, you will end up disappointing your fans and followers and jeopardizing your social marketing initiative."[5]

That said, the network effect associated with publishing content to multiple channels is significant. In Chapter 5 we looked at interactions and found that customers generated 152 interactions per post on average (based on awareness aggregate data). I looked at that same data through a slightly different lens. This time I focused on looking at interaction rates across multiple channels versus a single channel.

Content published on two or three channels had a 24 percent increase in engagement over content published to a single chan-

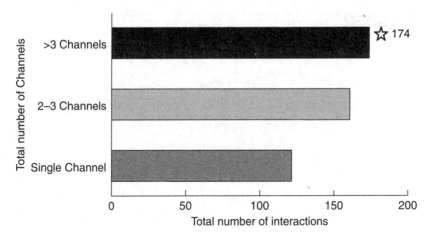

nel. *Content published to more than three channels had an increase in engagement of over 30 percent.*

Let me give you an example of how this works. Let's say you work at a software company and are promoting a new white paper. Depending on the size of your audience, you would get certain results posting to one social network, Facebook. If you took that same white paper, posted it on your company blog, tweeted a link to it, and promoted it on your Facebook page, your results would improve by somewhere around 24 percent. Additionally, if you also posted it to Scribd and Slideshare, your results would improve by 30 percent over just posting to Facebook alone.

Now, there are a lot of factors that play into this analysis: network size on each channel, how viral the document is, and most important, how *compelling* the content is. Jeremiah Owyang, industry analyst with Altimeter Group, advises "Content that people are willing to register for is content that helps them make better business decisions. If your content is good, you will see that, after a person consumes it, he or she is willing to share it and make it spread."[6]

CASE STUDY
MARKETO, B2B CONTENT MARKETING AT ITS BEST

Marketo is a provider of marketing automation software and is growing rapidly, thanks to a marketing engine the pumps out content to drive inbound sales inquiries.

A FOCUS ON CONTENT

Content produced by Marketo goes well beyond the development of white papers or blog posts. They utilize multiple types of content to generate leads as well as to help advance buyers through the sales process. Maria Pergollino, Senior Director of Marketing at Marketo, was recently quoted in a blog post discussing the company's philosophy on content marketing:

> It comes down to two things: risk mitigation and trust. Content helps purchasers mitigate risk. They can take a piece of content and go to their boss and say, "Look, here are examples of what others have done, and here's a white paper on why it works." It's all about getting the person to feel comfortable, as they're getting ready to buy.
>
> I want to make sure that when people are going to their boss with that content, it's got my logo on it. If all the research and information is from us, then it makes it very hard for a decision-maker to trust or recommend a competitor instead.[7]

Marketo leverages multiple types of content to drive prospects back to their home base. Content is distributed through a number of

channels, and social media destinations include their blog, Twitter, and Facebook. They also generate targeted content to make sure that prospects have the highest likelihood of becoming sale leads. Leads are nurtured in a three-week process where Marketo delivers regular content in order to stay in front of potential new clients. At the end of the 21-day lead nurturing program a final e-mail is sent giving options for recipient to self-score themselves in terms of their interest in Marketo.

One of the most interesting concepts employed by Marketo to automate this process is called "content mapping." This is a process of developing and mapping content that is relevant to where prospects are in the buying cycle. This helps move people through the buying process by deliberately serving content that is relevant to their specific needs and challenges.

Interested in learning more about content mapping? Marketo has produced an excellent resource call **"The B2B Content Marketing Cheat Sheet"** that provides details on how to map your content marketing program.

Marketo remains one of the fastest growing software companies in the market and credits much of that growth to a robust content marketing strategy.

TAKEAWAYS

- **Content mapping:** Map the right types of content into your outbound marketing programs to make sure you are giving the right content to the appropriate individuals, and at the right stage of the buying process.

- **Content syndication:** Don't simply send an e-mail linking to a good piece of content. Syndicate it out to multiple social destinations to maximize exposure to your audience.

- **Blog as your home base:** Blog about your content and direct your audience back to your home base to generate conversions.

FIVE STEPS FOR DEFINING A SOCIAL CONTENT STRATEGY

Building your own social-content strategy is a snap. We'll start by defining the types of contexts that are available to you, based on which kind of content is most effectively hosted on each individual channel. Then we'll move on to how you can assess your content assets. Finally, we'll look at ways to strategize content for multi-channel distribution.

STEP 1: DEFINE YOUR OUTPOSTS

One of the most important decisions you need to make, up front, is identifying the channels to which you want to publish content. That said, let's take a quick look into the different categories to which you can publish, depending on your audience.

1. **Blogs:** The most critical components of your social marketing strategy. Think of your blog as the foundation of your social content strategy. It should serve to aggregate all social content and stand as a centralized location for all content. Your blog should be your landing page and serve as a search engine–optimized resource for prospects to discover you and your company.

2. **The social networks:** Facebook, LinkedIn, and Google+ are the largest networks at the time this book goes to print. You will need to identify which ones are the best fit for your audience and use them as vehicles for publishing content. Establishing a consistent presence across networks is discussed in detail in Chapter 10. Once you have a robust presence established, the content sharing you drive across these networks is critical to getting people to view and engage with the information you have to offer.

3. **Twitter:** Building a large list of followers is a great way to meet people and increase traffic to your blog and websites.

4. **Social news:** Directories such as Digg, Reddit, and StumbleUpon serve as mechanisms to drive additional views to your content.

5. **Video:** As we learned earlier, people learn visually and video is a great method to support this. If you notice your audience enjoys video content, include video as a channel, and begin to develop content specifically for this.

6. **Photo sharing:** Flickr, Pinterest, Instagram, Photobucket, and others have emerged as key photo-sharing destinations. In addition to being a great location to generate engagement, they also serve as excellent outlets for SEO.

7. **Document sharing:** Sites like Scribd and Slideshare provide a powerful resource for individuals researching specific topics. Including content like white papers, e-books, and presentations on these sites will catch the eyes of individuals who are searching for your content.

There are hundreds of additional sites not mentioned above. The key is understanding where your audience is and syndicating content to those destinations and beyond to drive maximum exposure.

Olympus: Are You PEN Ready? A Case for Consumer-Generated Content

Michael Bourne is a Senior VP Account Director at Mullen, a full-service marketing agency integrating disciplines from creative to direct response, public relations, full-service media, social influence, digital production, and analytics. Michael is also the manager of the Olympus Imaging America, Inc., account, a long-standing client of Mullen's.

In September 2011, Olympus launched the PEN Ready Project, a campaign designed to promote the new Olympus PEN® E-PM1 camera by empowering and inspiring creativity in more than 1,000 individuals around North America. To demonstrate that anyone can be "PEN Ready," Olympus surprised people in undisclosed locations throughout New York City, Los Angeles, San Francisco, Toronto, Miami, and nearby its U.S. headquarters in Lehigh Valley, Pennsylvania, by giving them the Olympus PEN® E-PM1 camera. The images and HD videos that participants create with the camera as part of the PEN Ready Project are showcased on a custom-designed Olympus Tumblr blog at http://penready.com.

To give the program a suitable takeoff, Olympus partnered with JetBlue Airways, the un-airline for today's jet set, which shares a love of blue-sky ideas like the PEN Ready Project. On September 16, Olympus gave the PEN E-PM1 camera to unsuspecting JetBlue customers on a flight that departed New York's JFK International Airport bound for Florida.

Let's Give 'Em Something to Talk About

The goal for the second phase of the campaign was to ensure that it was highly participatory. Olympus knew that engagement on social media would be critical in order to pique interest and convert users. What better way to spread social media interest than to place the product directly in the hands of the consumers. The result? The largest camera giveaway in history.

The key to success was encouraging those who were "PEN Ready" to post their content online, and to get people to talk about their love of the camera. Olympus already had a site and an evolved presence on Facebook, Twitter, YouTube, Instagram, and Flicker. With a strong online community already established, they determined that the project merited its own platform to focus on the new camera line and serve as a digital hub for the campaign. Mullen and Olympus felt that Tumblr was the best option to accomplish the PEN Ready Project's goals, given the platform's high level of customization and capacity for users to like, blog, and reblog content as well as follow other bloggers for sharing and networking. In partnership with Tumblr, the new PEN Ready blog launched at the same time that the top 100 Tumblr bloggers received an E-PM1 camera of their own to create art for the site as well as for their own blogs.

As you can begin to see, content can be created in multiple ways. There's media coverage of the campaign. There's each and every Tumblr blogger who's sharing it through multiple pathways, and these active participants are super-sharers and project co-creators—as is everyone who views and reblogs the content. There are also influencers who share their perspective on the project,

things they've seen, and what they've liked about it, which is being heard by yet another audience. All of these outlets combine to make a powerful marketing impact.

The Power of Partnering with Your Biggest Fans

The icing on the cake with a campaign like the PEN Ready Project is when you truly connect with your product's biggest fans. Rarely, in the past, has marketing been able to share and generate enthusiasm in the way that companies can today.

Michael shared an e-mail that came directly from a PEN Ready Project participant whose involvement changed the way she saw the world:

Hello, I'm absolutely in love with the Pen Ready camera. My family now gets to call me the paparazzi. I've uploaded my pics to Facebook on your Get Olympus page. I know that this was a giveaway and people were chosen randomly, but your company has no idea how something that is a definite win-win both for the consumer and Olympus has completely changed my life in some very personal ways, and given me back what I thought I had lost: confidence, believing in myself. Thank you.

Overall, the connection that is being made between the consumers, the product, and the consumers' networks are very powerful.

RESULTS TO DATE

- 79 percent growth across all social platforms
- Over 30,000 photo submissions to PENReady.com
- Over 1.3 million consumer engagements with PEN Ready content
- Over 1 million YouTube video views
- 22,321,340 impressions on all social sites with PEN Ready content
- Over 622 million media impressions for the camera and campaign

Source: Data provided in a 2012 interview with Michael Bourne of Mullen.

Takeaways: Every channel is serving the needs of every other channel, so PENReady videos are on YouTube, tweets are directed to consumers on the streets, Flickr images are curated, Facebook posts share the experience, and Instagram influencers spread the word by using the camera to create. Beyond marketing directly to online influencers, the company proactively went outside to the streets and found everyday consumers to become brand advocates that actively promote the product and what it can do.

STEP 2: PERFORM A CONTENT INVENTORY AND AUDIT

Now that you've seen the breadth of channels you can publish to, it's time to determine the kind of content you want to distribute. Begin the process by taking inventory of the content you currently have. Most businesses have a lot of content to work with, and it's critical to understand what you have before understanding what it is you need.

A *content inventory* answers the question: *What do we have to work with?* It includes a detailed list of all documents (white papers, presentations, product manuals, etc.), video and audio assets, and images related to your business. This analysis serves as a quantitative measure of what you have.

A *content audit,* on the other hand, is an analysis of the information assets you have. It is the assessment of that content and an evaluation of its importance and relevance with the surrounding messaging. The content audit will answer the question: *Is this any good?*

Start by making a list of all the content you have on hand, by type of content, theme of content, and date published (if available). Your spreadsheet will look something like Table 7.1 (I borrowed this from the spreadsheet we use at Awareness).

Table 7.1 **Content Inventory Sample**

Type	Theme	Title	Date published
Video	Content marketing	Intro to Content Marketing with Joe Pulizzi	Jan 1, 2011
White paper	Best practices	Best Practices on Facebook	Feb 3, 2011
Product manual	Getting started guide	Getting started with our product	Feb 11, 2011
Blog	Social SEO	Getting the most out of Social with SEO	March 2, 2011
Webinar	Content marketing	Content Rules! with C.C. Chapman	March 13, 2011
E-Book	Social funnel	The Social Marketing Funnel	March 18, 2011
Video	Social media	Interview with Paul Gillin	March 28, 2011
Infographic	Social media	CMO Opinions	April 3, 2011

Once you have a complete inventory, look back at each piece of content and ask two questions:

1. **Is this content still relevant?**

   a. If no, can it be updated to be relevant?

   b. If yes, save it for future use?

2. **Is the topic still relevant?**

   a. If no, can it be rephrased or reworked?

   b. If yes, are there components that we can reuse in our marketing?

To help answer these questions, consider including some additional categories on your spreadsheet:

1. Short description

2. Interaction metrics: number of downloads, comments, shares, etc.

3. Pages that link to this page

Interested in getting a deeper dive in content marketing? Check out Joe Pulizzi's book *Get Content, Get Customers* and *Content Rules* by C.C. Chapman and Ann Handley.

STEP 3: DEVELOP A CONTENT-MARKETING PLAN AND GAP ANALYSIS

Now that you know what you have to start with, it's time to develop a content-marketing plan and perform a gap analysis to identify the content holes you need filled. The backbone of your content-marketing plan is an editorial calendar. It will contain a list of topics, types of content, and where each piece will be published over a specified period of time.

I recommend building your editorial calendar around themes and by month. At Awareness we have a content calendar that looks out over six months, driven by key product and market themes. Six months allow the right mix of planning and flexibility, depending on how content takes off or needs rescheduling.

Table 7.2 shows a very small snippet of the calendar we use internally and how we manage ongoing content programs.

Table 7.2 **Sample Content Management Worksheet**

Theme	Topic	Type	Drop date	Destination	Owner
Content marketing	Content marketing	Webinar	Jan. 5, 2011	Webinar	Lewis
Content marketing	Best practices	Blog	Jan. 6, 2011	Blog, landing page, FB, TW, LI	Lewis
Content marketing	Content marketing playbook	E-book	Jan. 8, 2011	Blog, landing page, e-mail, TW, FB, LI, SS	Giliberto

In reality, our calendar is much more detailed, so take note of the level of detail you need, based on your social-content–strategy needs. We identify each source for promotion as a line item to make sure we understand where and when things are being published. Here are the key areas to manage:

1. **Theme:** What is the overall theme of the content being published?

2. **Topic:** What is the specific topic we want to cover?

3. **Type:** What type of content is it?

4. **Drop date:** What day will the content drop?

5. **Destinations:** Where will it be promoted and published? Note: This includes promotional channels as well as sponsored e-mail blast, banner ad placements, and others.

6. **Owner:** Who is the owner of the specific piece of content?

With your editorial calendar in place, it's time to perform a content-gap analysis. In this phase you will compare the content you currently have with the content you need. Pay attention to types of content and which content has worked well in the past.

STEP 4: DEVELOP CONTENT

Developing the content you need may seem like the most straight-forward aspect of the program, when in fact it can be much more complex. Because each type of content is very different, I'm going to provide some tips on content development to help make the process easier.

1. **Six to one ratio:** Develop each piece of content with the idea that it should be distributable in six different ways. This is a policy we have implemented as part of our marketing system at Awareness, and it works very well. The premise is that any one piece of content can result in a minimum of four additional pieces of content. Let me explain with a specific example.

    Last year we developed an e-book call *The Social Marketing Funnel.* The e-book represented research of Awareness customers, as well as interviews with thought leaders and experts. The 30-page project was published in August 2011. As an offshoot of that piece we also developed 15 interviews with experts that were interviewed as research for the book, a live webinar, slides from the webinar, an infographic featuring a roadmap to social media, multiple blog posts, and a graphical version of the e-book.

    That one single e-book generated an additional 28 separate pieces of content. Let me give you the breakdown of where they were published and how they performed:

    a. **E-book:** Released on August 1, 2011. Promoted on Facebook, Twitter, the company blog, and through various sponsored e-mails. Generated over 5,800 downloads.

b. **Blog posts:** Series began on August 1, with 15 posts scheduled to take place. Blog posts accounted for 2,000 additional downloads of the full e-book.

c. **Infographic:** Posted on over 20 blogs, including high-traffic sites like AllTop, Socialnomics, and Social Times. Generated additional 3,000 downloads.

d. **Webinar and video:** Live webinar resulted in 1,000 registrations and 600 attendees. Video recording generated 1,000 additional views.

e. **Graphic e-book:** Posted to Slideshare and Scribd. Became a featured Slideshare presentation for a week. Generated over 35,000 views.

   That one single e-book generated additional content that allowed downloads to grow virally.

2. **Outsource:** Many companies attempt to develop all their content internally, but it can be daunting to look at the amount of content you need to develop. While you may have excellent resources on staff, in most cases outsourcing development can be a blessing. There are thousands of freelance writers, video producers, webinar transcribers, and other available professionals who offer their services at a very reasonable cost. Great places to find them include Mechanical Turk, Craigslist, and MediaBistro.

3. **Be nimble and ready for change:** The only guarantee you have in your industry is that hot topics will change. You need to be prepared and ready to embrace new topics as they arise and incorporate them into your editorial calendar. While you may

have a plan for six months, it should be viewed as extremely fluid. It will almost always need to be modified. I recommend a weekly review of your content plan and allowing your team to swap topics in and out as needed, to ensure that you are always putting your best foot forward.

STEP 5: DEPLOY, TEST, AND GROW

With your content in place it's time to begin deploying it and in accordance with the timeline developed in your content calendar. Start by deploying content to the destinations you outlined in Step 1. Don't be afraid to test content and make sure you have a measurement plan in place at each stage. Important things to look at include:

1. How engaging is the content?
2. Is it driving conversions?
3. Which content types generate the most engagement, conversions, views, etc.?
4. Which topics generate the most engagement, conversions, views, etc.?
5. Who are your most effective authors?
6. Which channels perform best? Which pieces of content perform best on each channel?

The bottom line is there are a lot of things to pay attention to when getting your content strategy on the right track. The more you analyze the performance of your content, the better your chance for success.

TIPS FOR CONTENT PLANNING

1. **Obey cross-platform rules of engagement:** As you start to publish across platforms, be very aware that content needs to be built for the platform on which you are publishing. For instance, the content you add to Facebook will be very different from what you post on your blog. Be sure to obey the rules of engagement for each destination to make sure you maximize your potential for success.

2. **Cross-platform consistency:** One of the common mistakes brands make is that their content varies too much from channel to channel. While content needs to be customized for the channel to which you are publishing, it's important to keep the messaging, the look, and the feel consistent.

3. **Know your customers and what they want:** As it is in every aspect of marketing, understanding the needs of your audience is critical. Before you begin publishing, get a deep understanding of who they are and what they need. Look at the other pieces of content they engage with, and use that as a baseline for identifying topics and content types that will resonate most with them.

4. **Workflow/approval process:** Larger companies and small companies will benefit by implementing a workflow process to make sure all content coming from the brand is consistent and on message. This especially helps if you are working with junior team members to make sure all content is checked for accuracy and consistency. More details about workflow process considerations can be found in Chapter 11.

5. **Micro-targeting:** Not all content should be developed for your entire audience. In many cases it's important to serve content to target segments of your fan base. For example, you may be running a sale at a store location in NYC. That certainly does not apply to your fans in LA. In Facebook, you can geo-target that content to NYC residents alone. In addition, you may want to target content based on language. If your followers are diverse enough, consider translating content into relevant languages such as Spanish, French, etc. and using language targeting in Facebook to serve that content to the appropriate market.

6. **Content curation:** David Meerman Scott, describes content curation on his blog. "An interesting aspect of the culture of sharing on social networks is that of content curation. Content curation is the act of pointing your followers to content from other people. Anyone who sometimes uses Twitter to send people to an interesting blog post, or news article, or video that they did not create is *curating* content. A retweet is a form of content curation too. Essentially the idea is that you find things that interest you, and you share them. If you become known as 'always finding the good stuff' people will eagerly follow you, even if you don't do much in the way of original content."[8]

    The point here is, don't feel like you need to create 100 percent original content. Be on the lookout for content that is relevant to your market and share it with your followers. This will increase the value you provide and will encourage more followers as you become a thought leader around a topic.

7. **Invest in systems:** There are a lot of things to consider as you develop a multi-channel social-content marketing strategy. To

make sure you have workflows and effective management in place, I strongly recommend investing in a system to help manage everything you do. A good SMMS (social media management system) will provide a centralized location for everyone to log in to as they publish and engage with content. It will also provide connections to each social destination you engage with, so you won't need to worry about publishing content to one place, only to copy it over and over again to other destinations. It will format the content for each channel and allow you to publish with a single click, as well as control workflows within your group.

THE IMPORTANCE OF CONTENT-RICH LANDING PAGES AND BLOGS FOR CONVERSION

What the results above demonstrate is the importance of having a destination where your content lives outside of the social web, so you can take advantage of the power of SEO.

Search engine optimization, the process of creating and optimizing website content that shows up in Google's top search results, is among the top areas of social marketing investment for companies of all sizes. Social Media Examiner's 2011 Report highlights increased traffic (72 percent) and improved search rankings (62 percent) among the top benefits of social media marketing.[9]

Effective search engine optimization involves tying strategic keywords to specific website pages and, increasingly, to targeted landing pages. These targeted landing pages can be used to drive both organic traffic from search engine results and traffic from your social media channels, offering a natural continuation to the dialog started on the social web.

Landing pages become the social glue that ties the social to traditional marketing, helping companies realize lead generation and sales return on their social marketing investment. Paul Gillin, the author of *Secrets of Social Media Marketing* and *The New Influencers*, advises that: "For B2B companies, the most effective way to drive lead generation is through search optimization, because of the long tail effect. Many B2B companies offer specialized services for which there is a limited domain of keywords people use."[10]

The core of a company's social strategy should be a blog or destination where content is published.

The benefits of using targeted landing pages are numerous:

- Landing pages offer more content control for complete and flexible messaging, media, and design than social media platforms such as Facebook and Twitter, which have limited messaging and commenting opportunities;

- Landing pages are aligned to keywords that clearly match the specific interests of prospects and customers; and

- Landing pages also allow for custom messaging and calls to action related to social sharing, "liking," commenting, and other ways of fueling word-of-mouth.

In addition to interactions, landing page popularity is driven by this channel's ability to popularize content within search engines. Success in this case can be measured by the number of inbound links generated to them—links from other reputable websites to your landing pages that help both drive qualified traffic and increase your online credibility.

Christine Major, corporate communications manager at Demandware, concurs: "One of the key ways we measure success at Demandware is the number of inbound links to our website. Growth in inbound links means we are creating relevant and useful content of interest to our industry."[11]

ACTIONS AND TAKEAWAYS

- Define your outposts, and tie your outposts to your home base.

- Develop content that can be distributed in multiple ways and on different channels.

- Use content inventories, audits, and gap analyses to structure your content market plan. Build flexibility into your expectations and schedules.

- The number of outlets to which you publish makes a difference on the impact your content can have.

- Deploy, test, and grow your strategy; delivering or curating content online to ensure success requires trial and error. Test what works and adjust your strategy accordingly.

CHAPTER 8

Stand Out Presence

Your brand's social presence is both the first and ongoing impression of your brand online. It incorporates your brand persona, the overall look and feel of your social destinations, the content you provide, and the engagement you offer. It is, simply stated, the overall experience your brand offers to your audience on the social web.

Your social presence cannot be understated: It can literally make or break your company's success in social marketing. How you structure and manage this presence will define how your audience views you and the type of engagement you will receive.

TRIPADVISOR: A STAND OUT SOCIAL PRESENCE

Before traveling most of us seek travel advice from friends and family who have visited the area previously. We inquire about "mustsee" attractions, favorite sights, places to eat, where to stay, and any other aspect of their experiences that can make our trip more enjoyable for us. We rely on advice and recommendations from those we trust to get insights into what we should do in order to get the most out of our vacation.

Automating this process is the objective of the online travel service, **TripAdvisor**. In an effort to develop a stand out experience for their users, the site www.tripadvisor.com incorporates

Facebook connect functionality into the site layout, to make a more compelling and personalized experience for their end users. When a user signs in with her Facebook credentials the site is immediately customized to feature the reviews and postings of Facebook friends.

The instant display of friends' reviews and opinions allows users to get content and recommendations based on the individuals they trust most. Most important, this helps define a unique experience for TripAdvisor users. It offers a unique and engaging presence that spans multiple social destinations and ties in directly to their corporate site. In addition to the Facebook customization, TripAdvisor maintains an independent and coordinated social media presence across the most popular social media destinations including Facebook, Twitter, Google+, and more.

The addition and integration of this functionality led TripAdvisor to see:

- Since TripAdvisor launched its Facebook integration, 57 million users have personalized their planning via the social network and 1.5 billion Facebook places pins have been placed by TripAdvisor users.

- In terms of page views per session TripAdvisor users via Facebook are 27 percent more engaged than average TripAdvisor users.

- Users connecting to TripAdvisor via Facebook were twice as likely to contribute content as those who connected via other means.[1]

The case of TripAdvisor shows us that a seamless presence makes a big difference. Once on TripAdvisor, fans and consumers immediately get the added value TripAdvisor has been able to generate through their social presence. Not only do consumers get it, but they also keep coming back.

YOU NEVER GET A SECOND CHANCE TO MAKE A FIRST IMPRESSION

The reason your audience will like and follow your brand on the social web is the same reason they follow you in the offline world. On the social web, as on the street, your presence can mean everything. It's the first impression your audience will have with your brand and is your basis for interaction. How it looks and how it feels will immediately give your audience an impression of who you are and what you are trying to do.

Take a moment and think about your favorite Facebook page. Something inspired you to like it. It's likely that you monitor the page in your Facebook feed and occasionally visit the page itself to view relevant content. For most people, the preference we have for the brands we follow across social media varies, depending on interests, which tend to change over time. For example, sometimes I pay attention to a specific company, like Apple, Delta, or Marvel. Other times it's a sports team, usually the Celtics, Bruins, Red Sox, or Patriots, depending on the season. Other times it's a TV show, movie, or other page that is entertainment related, like *Lost, Walking Dead, Howard Stern,* or *The Avengers.* The biggest thing these pages have in common is that the content is relevant to me, the reader, and I like to keep going back.

Before the relevancy of content, however, these pages all display very specific characteristics that help differentiate the page in the eyes of new fans.

Think about what your favorite page looks like, how it is structured, and how content is presented. As you review the page in your mind, elevate your thinking and consider the elements that make that page successful at first glance.

In this chapter we'll assess the ways that brands can develop their social media presence so that it is differentiated enough to separate it from the pack, gain new followers, and garner the highest results. To start, let's review the six rules you can implement to make your first impression a memorable one.

RULE 1. DEVELOP YOUR SOCIAL BRAND PERSONA

Your audience will make decisions on your brand based on what they see. They judge your outward appearance, a decision that likely takes place within seconds of coming to your social destination. Your social media persona exemplifies your brand values and mission, and both should be channeled cleanly into the look and feel of your site.

ASOS: BUILDING A SOCIAL PERSONA

With more than 1.7 million Facebook fans and 300 thousand Twitter followers, the UK-based fashion retailer ASOS.com is one of the most admired brands in the fashion industry. In their social media following, **ASOS** has created a brand persona that defines the image of their company: trendy, fashionable, customer focused, and socially responsible. It's clear, even from their early start in social media, that their aim was to develop a consistent and unified brand reflecting their mission.

Their initial foray into social media was the creation of an elaborate online community called ASOSLife. This area acted as the hub for fashion fans to communicate between one another and with ASOS directly. Users had the ability to set up their own blogs as part of the community. It also featured a forum where users could start their own threads, and it included an "ideas" section where users could suggest ideas to the ASOS team and get their ideas ranked by other users. This was carried into every other major social network including Facebook, Bebo, Twitter, Flickr, and others.

What is most impressive is that employees have always had the ability to speak on behalf of the brand, although it's clear that they are instructed to stay within corporate guidelines as they communicate with the audience. Employees who participate on social media add ASOS to the start of their Twitter handle (i.e. @ASOS_James) and tweet with customers regularly on behalf of the company. As a result, tweets and posts have individual personality while remaining consistent to the brand's overall messaging and strategy.

Taken all together, ASOS's brand persona and image are carried into the style of all their social destinations, including blogs, Facebook, and Twitter, as well as into the interactions that customers have with all employees. By taking this customer-centric approach ASOS has been able to connect with customers in a unique and personal way and it has helped them grow to become "the most loved digital brand in the UK."[2]

Like ASOS, brands need to take their social media personas very seriously and make sure their social brands accurately represent their identities, mission, values, and intent. The goal is to allow consumers to size up your brand quickly and entice them to engage immediately. Engagement is the critical next step, because your ultimate goal is to make the page worth coming back to on multiple occasions.

■

Takeaway: Most marketers do an excellent job of understanding the persona of their end customers. On the flip side,
most do not do enough to define and manage the persona
of their brand on social media. This is critical in the world of
social media marketing, where you may only have seconds to
gain a fan or follower. The key is to map out what you want
your brand persona to be *before* jumping into the social web,
and to make sure that the brand persona is carried through
every aspect of your social presence.

■

RULE 2. HUMANIZING YOUR BRAND'S SOCIAL PERSONA

Typically, brands approach social media as another channel to
broadcast their message. This broadcast approach has taken
brands away from dialog with end customers and has resulted in
the organization appearing more "non-human."

Humanizing your brand can have a profound impact on your
overall social media presence. Amy Jo Martin, founder of Digital
Royalty, is a master at humanizing brand presences on social
media. Her company works with brands like DoubleTree, Fox
Sports, Nike, and personalities like Dwayne "The Rock" Johnson,
Shaquille O'Neil, and UFC's Dana White to improve their social
media presence and humanize their brands. The key to her success is developing brand personas that engage with their audiences

and speak to followers on an individual level. UFC has grown to become incredibly popular and their fan base continues to grow. Their CEO is Dana White, a charismatic and aggressive promoter who has amassed over 2 million followers on Twitter. The reason for Dana's overwhelming following is his ability to both engage with his audience and humanize his personal brand, in addition to humanizing the UFC brand.

Here is a recent blog post from Amy on her work with Dana White and UFC:

Dana White, President of Ultimate Fighting Championship (disclosure: a Digital Royalty client), who has more than 1.5 million followers on Twitter and a global combined brand reach of more than 10 million via social media, offers value in the form of accessibility and providing exclusive, breaking news. He bridges the virtual and physical worlds by using platforms like Twitter and Facebook to meet fans in person or sharing his phone number with millions. The UFC is saving money, historically spent on advertising, because the company has built direct communication channels with high volume reach to their audience.[3]

The genius of Dana White is his ability to make himself approachable to the millions of fans who follow his sport. A key takeaway is creating that dialog with your fans. Migrate from the broadcast approach, and speak with your audience individually, allowing your brand to be more approachable, reachable, and respected.

RULE 3. BE CONSISTENT: DEVELOP A UNIFIED CROSS-PLATFORM PRESENCE

The most basic, yet probably the most important, thing you can do as you create your social media presence is to make sure it is consistent across every channel that you engage in. The average company has multiple unique social media outposts that they manage. This includes social outposts like Facebook, blogs, Twitter, YouTube, Flickr, LinkedIn, etc. as well as landing pages and websites.

Your unified cross-platform presence starts with the look and feel of your primary website and any auxiliary sites where you have established your presence, starting with your blog.

MASHABLE: BUILDING CONSISTENCY FROM THE CORE

Mashable is the largest independent news source dedicated to covering digital culture, social media, and technology. Their primary presence, or home base, is their website, mashable.com. They syndicate news through platforms including Facebook, Twitter, Google+, Pinterest, and others. A key to their success is that their online presence is consistent. The message, brand, look, and feel are all consistent to the brand's identity.

Mashable's social channels

RULE 4. YOUR PRESENCE NEEDS TO GRAB YOUR AUDIENCE RIGHT AWAY

The first objective of your social presence and the destinations you manage across the social web is to gain additional followers. If a visitor to your destination follows your brand, you can then message them in a one-to-one fashion. If the visitor likes or comments on something, that's great, but if he goes away without becoming a follower, he may not return. Your mission is to grab them right away, hook them on following you, and then engage with them directly.

ORANGE ENGAGES QUICKLY

Orange recently launched a program designed to build their audience quickly. A post to the HubSpot blog summarizes the program:

> British Telecommunications company Orange dramatized its Twitter followers' summer plans by giving them the summer blockbuster voiceover treatment. All Twitter users had to do was include #thissummer in their tweets along with their plans, and Orange would capture it and give some lucky followers the voiceover effect. Orange hosted the voiceovers on its blog, which helped generate more traffic to their site. Not only did this keep followers engaged with the brand, but it was fun, shareable, and in line with the brand's communication image.[4]

How many social media messages will you see today? Chances are, if you log in to Twitter or Facebook, you will be bombarded with actions and conversations from your friends' feeds. As marketers, this means we are in a constant battle for the attention of our audience. More important, we need to grab their attention quickly or risk losing them to the noise of the social web.

Here are some quick tips to maximize your ability to get your audience's attention right away.

TIP 1. KNOW YOUR AUDIENCE

With so much information available about your audience, there is no excuse for not offering content and experiences that they will enjoy and find valuable. Spend time up front studying your target audience, so that you know what type of content they want and what will get them to stick around.

TIP 2. USE VISUALS

Visuals are the first thing people will see. If they find the visuals compelling, they will move on to exploring your content in more detail.

TIP 3. CREATE A VELVET-ROPE ENGAGEMENT WITH EXCLUSIVE CONTENT

Grab your audience with the promise of exclusive content. Encourage first-time users to like your page, follow your tweets, or subscribe to your blog in exchange for offering outstanding content they would not receive as passive observers. This velvet-rope experience let's people know they are in a special club, and it inspires them to come back to see what else you have to offer.

TIP 4. USE MULTIPLE OFFERS

The same offers won't work on everyone in your audience. Expand the chances for engagement by offering multiple offers through multiple mediums. For example, you may have video content to serve through YouTube and special (though related) content on your twitter account.

RULE 5. DRIVE TO HOME BASE

Earlier I discussed the concept of "home base," which was introduced by Chris Brogan in 2008. Your home base is your primary online residence, the place where you direct the traffic from your outposts. Relative to your home base, online outposts represent "touch points away from your main online presence where you connect with others in some way."[5]

Businesses should structure under the same framework. While you will communicate and engage across many outposts, it's important to direct traffic back to your home base. Your home base should be in the form of a blog, a landing page, or your corporate website. Why this is so critical is because of Social SEO. Your home base will serve as the collection point for all your activity and will be optimized for SEO. In addition, it serves as a mechanism for conversion events, which you can track. Those conversion events are page views, downloads, or sales, and they are much more easily tracked on a destination you control.

RULE 6. MAKE YOUR PRESENCE A SOCIAL EXPERIENCE

Red Bull is an outstanding example of a brand that has created a dynamic, and one of the few brands that has truly adopted and integrated social media into their mix and has extended well beyond a traditional social media presence to build an outstand-

ing experience for their audience. Let's take a closer look at their Facebook presence alone to illustrate what I mean.

Mashable called Red Bull's fan page "easily one of the best on Facebook, simply because it has been able to break out of the typical fan page mold by providing fun content that encourages fans to interact with and ultimately connect with the brand."[6]

Red Bull has over 28 million fans who interact with, and are passionate about, the content the brand produces. Why is their page so special?

1. **It starts with the content:** The Red Bull page offers fans multiple types of content to engage any member of the audience. Games, videos, pictures, text are all well produced and on message. The messaging is straightforward, simple, and designed to appeal to their target audience.

2. **A fun experience:** Red Bull engages their fans by creating a fun experience. Red Bull offers a gaming center called the Red Bull Arcade as part of their Facebook page that rivals the likes of Zynga. They provide multiple games and other fun ways for fans to interact with the brand.

Several brands jump into social media without thinking about how it will affect their overall marketing strategy. Red Bull adopted the approach of developing an experience for their fans to make their presence engaging and interactive, with results in terms of brand awareness that is off the charts.

TAKING IT SOCIAL OFF THE NETWORKS

Those of you that believe social media is limited to the confines of Facebook, Twitter, YouTube, etc. could not be more wrong. The examples of brands like TripAdvisor, Red Bull, Levi's, and many others demonstrate that social media can, and should, be integrated throughout your online presence to be effective. This includes wrapping it into your corporate website.

Jeremiah Owyang recently published a post that discusses how brands should incorporate social media into their own corporate websites. He developed a matrix that allows any organization to see how to integrate social media into their online presence, based on the benefits they are seeking. See Jeremiah's Matrix in Table 8.1.

BE DELIBERATE: USE THIS ROAD MAP FOR YOUR WEB STRATEGY

Use this guide to map your current situation and where you plan to go. Copy and paste the framework into your corporate planning deck and identify where your assets are now. Get actionable by taking these three steps:

1. **Take inventory of your current corporate website assets.** Social media strategists must determine what level of sophistication they are at now and document their standing in their project plans. Take inventory of all corporate web assets and tag what already exists within this framework.

2. **Identify what the desired state is and then build a plan to reach it.** Note that the more you increase in sophistication, the more resources and stakeholder buy-ins are needed. Start small and slow, and be sure to have a strategy as you move forward.

3. **Don't arbitrarily jump into the social marketing space without measurable Key Performance Indicators (KPIs).** Be deliberate in your actions. Indicate on paper what the measurable

Table 8.1 Matrix: Evolution of Social Media Integration and Corporate Websites

Sophistication	Example	Benefit	Challenge
1. Do nothing, no social integration	Corporate websites that have no integration with social tools.	Cheap. Ignorance is bliss, at least in the short term	Your corporate website is irrelevant.
2. Link directly away without a strategy	Corporate homepages	Encourages growth of social channels that have chicklets that say "Follow us on Twitter/Facebook/YouTube/" sending traffic away. See share this, add this, and tweet-meme	Sending traffic away, without having a strategy
3. Link away, but encourage them to share with a pre-populated message	A chicklet that encourages new Twitter followers to tweet at their friends "I'm now following X brand"	Triggers a social alert as a form of endorsement	Better than the above, it may not have a follow-up or call to action
4. Brand experience is integrated in social channels	Extending the brand experience to social channels, so the corporaton is somewhat mirrored on social channels	Regardless of wherever users go, they are still experiencing the brand	Social channels sometimes serve better as a conversational area, not for traditional branding campaigns

(continued on next page)

Table 8.1 Matrix: Evolution of Social Media Integration and Corporate Websites *(continued)*

Sophistication	Example	Benefit	Challenge
5. Aggregating the discussion on your site	Aggregating select conversations from tweets as the Skittles homepage did, top discussions in communities or blogs. See Disqus and Echo	Centralizes the discussion on your site, making it a resource to first look at. Low-cost content.	Lack of control over which content can be created, still links off-site
6. Social log-in system that allows users to stay on-site	Using FB connect or Twitter connect allows users to use their existing log-ins to access the site. See how JanRain and Gigya (client) helps	May increase sign-ups, widening marketing tunnel, chances are content is more accurate than a sign-up form	May not have access to e-mail addresses, as users pass through using social log-ins.
7. Social login system that allows users to stay on-site, but triggers viral loop	In addition to the above, there's an actual social or interactive experience on the corporate site that triggers them to share with their friends	Users stay on-site, interact with brand or peers, yet recruit other members in social networks	Requires planning, a campaign, and extensive resources.
8. Complete integration between corporate site and social sites	Other than URLs there's no difference between a corporate site and a social site, the experience is seamless	Customers, prospects, and employees mix together, churning new members and viral activity	It doesn't exist, yet

Source: Owyang, Jeremiah, "Matrix: Evolution of Social Media Integration and Corporate Websites," WebStrategy Blog, March 28, 2010. http://www.web-strategist.com/blog/2010/03/28/matrix-evolution-of-integration-of-social-media-and-corporate-websites/.

goals are and how they'll tie back to business metrics. Relevant goals include increasing brand awareness, increasing leads, or increasing site conversions.[7]

Incorporating your social media platforms deeply into your web presence can require significant resources; however, you'll find that your interaction and conversion rates can grow significantly.

ACTIONS AND TAKEAWAYS

- Establish a brand persona. This means choosing a look and feel for each channel that reflects your brand's values and mission.

- Maintaining consistency across platforms will ensure that your presence is unified and is immediately recognizable by your target market.

- Grab attention right away to increase the numbers of people willing to follow you for the longer term.

- Take into consideration that the best brands develop a social experience through the content that they produce. With the resources available in today's market, you have the power and ability to produce highly engaging content. There's nothing stopping you from digging in deeply and producing a social experience that your followers will want to share.

CHAPTER 9

Stand Out Management

Managing and organizing the back-end processes of your social-marketing program is one of the biggest challenges businesses face. Your approach will help to reinforce the objectives of your social media strategy, guide the policies you put in place, and drive the roles you define for your team. Without proper structure from the beginning it will be impossible to develop a *stand out* strategy.

Throughout the previous chapters we have touched upon multiple aspects of management. This chapter consolidates those principles and serves as a guide to developing your management structure, strategy, and process.

A COMMON CHALLENGE

The rapid adoption of social media presents huge logistical headaches as organizations begin to structure teams around managing the process.

For most companies, participation in social media begins with only a few social media–savvy employees. They begin (primarily on their own) to develop outposts on multiple social networks. Their work tends to represent a grassroots effort within the company, initiated by individuals, groups, or departments who recognize the power of social media for the business overall. Participation is typically not a coordinated effort, and these efforts are seldom integrated into any marketing mix or overarching business objectives, at least initially.

As businesses mature and put more focus on social media marketing, they typically begin by naming an individual within the company as the owner of the company's social strategy. Nine out of ten times, this person has a job with other responsibilities, and social media represents only a small percentage of his or her overall set of responsibilities. This presents a challenge for the individual in charge, because social media is a 24-7 job. These individuals usually come to realize two extremely important facts about social media. First, they realize that, despite perception, social media is not for free and requires resources to be successful. Second, they realize that a business's approach to social media is very different from the approach an individual takes. More often than not, the individual in charge quickly realizes that he or she is resource-constrained and needs help to effectively address the social-media management challenges that he or she faces—in terms of both people and infrastructure.

As businesses begin organizing around social media, whether they are just starting out or are beginning to reorganize their overall strategy, there are four areas worth paying particular attention to in order to get it right:

1. Building a stand out team

2. Defining a stand out process

3. Implementing stand out policies and guidelines

4. Designing a stand out system

BUILDING A STAND OUT TEAM

Whether your team is diving in for the first time or restructuring an existing strategy so that it becomes more effective, you should aim to answer the following questions as you build out your social media team.

1. What are your business objectives, and how do they tie in to your overall social marketing strategy?

2. To accomplish these objectives, which departments and individuals need to be involved in your social-marketing efforts?

As we discussed in earlier chapters, setting objectives for your social media strategy is critical. Some goals might include:

- **Building buzz:** To increase excitement about your brand
- **Driving sales:** To increase sales numbers and leads
- **Customer service:** To resolve customer-service issues through social channels
- **Brand awareness:** To gain followers and fans
- **Customer support:** To communicate more effectively with users about your brand
- **Getting opinions:** To learn more about what users think of your brand

Your objective in social media should align with your overall business objectives. Once you have a list of goals, you can begin to identify the best people to help you accomplish them. Be aware that this list may result in objectives that touch multiple departments and job functions. How to cope with any gray area in terms of delegation is what I want you to gain from the following sections and case studies.

WHO SHOULD JOIN OUR SOCIAL MEDIA TEAM?

As discussed in earlier chapters, anyone from the CEO to the intern can be involved in your social media efforts. To reiterate, there are typically three common places to recruit for your social media team:

1. **The marketing department:** This is the obvious first stop for social media talent. If your company has an in-house marketing staff, they should already be abreast of the latest social media trends. In well-developed marketing departments they should also have the resources necessary to execute sound strategies for engaging with consumers and creating quality content.

2. **The call center:** If your company already has a team that handles customer complaints and questions, they should continue to perform this duty with additional social media training. They should also be encouraged to help the company develop new ways of serving customers using social media. Your call-center team may also be motivated to participate by the fact that social media allows companies to post useful information, enabling customers to answer common questions for themselves—which actually decreases call-center workload.

3. **An outside public-relations firm or agency:** Companies big and small often bring in additional help to gain expertise, as well as gain access to relationships their company does not currently have.

MANAGING WORKFLOW AUDIT TRAILS AND PERMISSIONS

The team executing your social media strategy may be decentralized or cross-departmental and may have different core areas of focus during their participation (service versus sales versus marketing). Developing a workflow process behind the scenes to help organize who is responsible for each interaction is important to make sure everyone is on the same page.

The good news is that, departmentally, objectives typically dictate the types of engagements each group is responsible for.

- **Customer service:** Focused on resolving customer issues. Their primary role is listening and responding to issues as they arise.

- **Sales:** Focused on dealing with sales inquiries that arise from social channels.

- **Marketing:** Responsible for generating demand and running promotions.

- **PR and corporate communications:** Responsible for branding and managing corporate communications.

JETBLUE: FOCUSED MANAGEMENT AND SUCCESS

One of the best examples of management on the social web is JetBlue. Take a look at a sample of their Twitter feed over the period of one hour (picture is courtesy of Erik Qualman, @equalman).

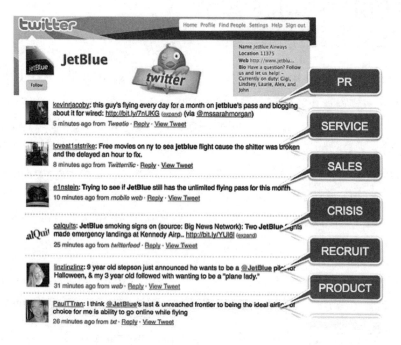

Notice that, in that one-hour period, they received tweets that required different departments within the company to take notice and respond. JetBlue's work process behind the scenes ensures that the tweets are routed to the appropriate team members for follow-up. This is an excellent example of a company that has organized and centralized their social media efforts.

SETTING ACCESS AND PERMISSIONS

Not everyone on your team has the same roles and responsibilities in relation to your social media presence. Managing how different team members can access it can become a big issue. For many companies, access to social media is controlled by an excel spreadsheet that houses the passwords for every social destination that the company is involved in. In the worst case, this represents a huge security hole, as most spreadsheets are not encrypted and passwords can be stolen.

In addition, it does not allow you to control the type of access each individual gets within each channel. For example, you may decide to have your customer-service team only respond to comments on your Facebook page, but they can't publish content. Maybe they are only limited to interacting on Facebook. Setting controls can be easy with a Social Marketing Management (SMMS) software package that allows you to define the permissions for each user.

WORKFLOW

A good workflow process will incorporate two components: managing approvals for outgoing messages and outlining ownership and follow-up for inbound messaging.

For outgoing messages an approval process may be required before each post goes live. For example, you may have an intern or an agency draft content to publish through social media channels and then have that content go through an automated approval process before it's published in order to reduce the chance of inappropriate messaging getting out. In highly regulated industries it can become important for legal to view content before it goes out.

For inbound messaging, the key is prioritizing the messages, assigning them to the appropriate person for follow-up, and making sure responses are prompt. For example, you need to make sure customer-service issues are routed to someone in the company who can resolve them. Your team captain can help manage this process initially, but depending on volume, you will likely need to implement a system that will help you manage the back-end process. A system that allows you to flag or set statuses once someone has responded to a comment is critical in order to do this.

Your team leader should play a vital role in managing workflow, but it may not be realistic to expect him or her to do everything for everyone. It may work best to split up the task list by department and then charge the team leader with keeping each department informed of the others' efforts.

Some examples of task distribution include:

- Charge your marketing team with monitoring brand-based conversations and creating blog posts, which are approved by the COO, while you leave responding to customers up to the customer-service team. Meet regularly with the team leader to discuss each department's progress in resolving issues and engaging fans.

- Assign the content creation to the creative department. Charge the team leader with editing and posting all content, ask the engineering department to handle gathering metrics on user response, and share all information by e-mail.

- Require every member of the team to log-in to social media daily and generate a memo on his or her area of expertise.

Content assignments can also be assigned, which can be approved by the team leader for online posting.

Of course, in some small companies there may be one person doing most, if not all, of this work. Using a social media tracking program can be very helpful in this regard; if you're an art-school grad being charged to deliver analytics from three different social media networks, smart software beats a messy Excel sheet any day of the week.

▮

Are you a CMO looking for more advice? Check out this presentation called **"The Social Marketing Roadmap"** featuring advice from leading social-marketing experts.

▮

MANAGING WORKFLOW AT THE SUPER BOWL XLVI SOCIAL MEDIA COMMAND CENTER

With thousands of people converging on Indianapolis for Super Bowl XLVI, the **Super Bowl Host Committee** relied on social media to manage interactions with fans and visitors who were in town for the big day. They constructed the Social Media Command Center, which was staffed by 46 avid social-media experts from Indiana, who worked side-by-side with a staff of 50, including student interns from nearby universities, to make the Super Bowl XLVI a memorable and safe experience. The team monitored more than 300 keywords on Facebook, Twitter, YouTube, and Flickr. CNN reported this week that the team "will tweet directions to fans in search of parking, direct visitors to Indianapolis's best attractions, and stand by to provide information in case of a disaster."

As you can imagine, this is a gigantic undertaking and a key to the success was implementing a software solution to manage the workflow behind the interactions with fans. The team had the ability to monitor comments in real time, assign tasks to individuals for follow-up, track who responded to which comments, and manage a complete approval process on all interactions.

Want to learn more about the metrics generated by the Super Bowl Host committee during Super Bowl XLVI? Check out this great Super Bowl Infographic created by Raidious over at the blog.

As a result, the Social Media Command Center generated over $3.2 million in value through amplified social reach and engagement, with an estimated 64 million impressions at kickoff alone.[1]

ACCOUNTABILITY

As more and more individuals within your company participate on the social web, it becomes critical to track who said what, where, and when. Audit trails have become a priority at companies large and small. This is particularly important at publicly traded companies and within highly regulated industries such as financial services, pharmaceuticals, and health care.

Managing an audit trail to track all your engagements is important for a number of reasons, but the number one reason is for accountability. As a manager of social media strategy, it is critical for you to be able to understand which comments were made by which employees, and when. Having this system in place will force employees to think twice before posting content to make sure it's within company policies and guidelines.

GETTING YOUR TEAM ON SCHEDULE

After you have decided on a workflow that distributes tasks appropriately among team members you should aim to create a content calendar, with deadlines and tasks outlined for each project. Your team's overall goal should be to *produce great content as often as you can, with the resources available.*

The social media world is always changing, so resist the urge to cling to a six-month-old strategy that's not working. But at the same time, resist the urge to abandon ship too soon on a social media project that hasn't existed long enough to gather useful metrics on user response and return on investment (ROI). Instead, aim for a middle ground in which your team develops a social media strategy that has:

- Deadlines that challenge your staff and that keep content timely, without making unreasonable demands on their time or energy.

- Workflow that allows enough time to properly complete each step of the process.

- Regular meetings to review upcoming projects and user response to past projects.

- Beginning and end date for your strategy, after which your team will evaluate ROI and make appropriate changes to the workflow and calendar.

Here's an example of a how a content calendar interacts with the team's workflow. Say your company's working on a new promotional video. Your content calendar will outline:

- Who will create the video from beginning to end

- Who will post about the video on Facebook and Twitter

- Who will respond to comments about the video

- Who will generate reports about the traffic and response to the video

- What are the expected deadlines for each task

THE BASICS OF POLICIES AND GUIDELINES

Putting in place a set of policies or guidelines that keeps everyone on the same page can be the difference between a successful social strategy and one that is doomed from the start. A solid policy and set of guidelines will allow your team to have a clear overview of what is expected of them and ensure that everyone is on the same page. With these in place, differentiating how your brand interacts on the social web becomes much easier.

POLICY IN ACTION: SOCIAL MEDIA AND THE 2012 OLYMPICS

The International Olympic Committee (IOC) understands the global power of social media and is encouraging athletes participating in the 2012 Olympic Games to post updates on blogs, Facebook, and Twitter. While the Committee understands the positive effect social media can have, they also understand that, if used inappropriately, it can have negative repercussions. Therefore they have issued social media, blogging, and Internet guidelines for Olympians, with a warning that those who break the rules risk being thrown out of the Games.

Mitch Wagner, Editor in Chief of TheCMOSite.com discusses why the policy that the IOC put in place is a good one:

> You don't need a legal degree to understand it, and you don't have to set aside a whole day to read it. The entire document is four pages. With big fonts. And wide margins. Written in plain language. It takes five minutes to read.
>
> If your social media guidelines are very long, and are packed with legalese, no one will read them. The document will simply be ignored. Nobody will get in trouble for violating the social media policy, because even the managers responsible for enforcing the policy won't bother to read it.[2]

The guidelines presented to athletes include the following:

- No commercial or advertising use, meaning athletes cannot promote their personal sponsors, which could be seen or defined as an ambush of competitors or guerilla marketers.

- Athletes may not report on competitions.

- Athletes may not report information that's "private in nature" about other competitors or accredited persons.

- Athletes must not post vulgar or obscene content.

- Athletes must not post any audio or video from within the Olympic venues; however, they can post photos of themselves.

- There are also restrictions on posts using the logo of the Olympic rings.

- The IOC has, in general, advised athletes to use social media responsibly and at their own risk.

■

Like the IOC, businesses need to prepare all employees who can access the social web for positive and proper interactions they will have with constituents. They need a detailed understanding of what is acceptable, and what is not, as they represent your brand online.

Taking a two-pronged approach to policies helps to address both the legal and behavioral concerns a business has with regards to employees participating in social media. The first step is to implement a set of formal, legal policies that are rolled out to the entire company. These policies should also be incorporated into relevant employee documents (handbooks, etc.). The second step is to implement a set of guidelines that outline the social media culture and expected behavior during interactions. Structured in this way, policies are more focused on legal issues, and guidelines are more focused on marketing.

YOUR SOCIAL MEDIA POLICY

As you create your social media policy, don't be afraid to borrow key points from companies who already have social media policies developed and shared online. Companies such as Coca-Cola, Kodak, and IBM have developed comprehensive and efficient social media policies that they have made available for sharing.

As you review the components of different social media policies, there are several things you should be sure to include.

THE LEGALESE

I am not an attorney, nor do I play one on TV, so please consult counsel before implementing any of the following advice.

Legal aspects of your policy will typically include:

- **Confidentiality:** You want to make sure that a staff member doesn't take to the social web to prematurely announce an acquisition your company is making. This section will specifically outline what can and can't be shared via social media, and it will advise staff on what constitutes proprietary information within your company.

- **Industry-specific laws:** Some industries, such as pharma, health care, or financial services, have a specific set of rules that need to be taken into account as you communicate on the social web. Be sure to detail these specific requirements and laws for employees, so that they fully understand how these requirements will affect their overall participation in social media.

ESTABLISHING THE CODE OF SOCIAL CONDUCT

It's important for employees to understand the overall code of conduct for participation within social media. This code outlines the expectations for behavior of every employee who participates in the social web. Some areas to focus on include:

- **Formal disclosures:** Outline how employees should identify themselves as part of your company when they participate in online conversations. Associations with the company should be included within their bios on every social network they participate in. Additionally, they should also disclose anytime they are talking about a client or partner and promoting their business.

- **Training and resources:** Outline specific training that needs to take place before engaging in social media on behalf of the company. Identify any resources they need to review prior to engaging.

- **Time allocation:** Enabling your employees to participate in social media at a reasonable level during work hours is encouraged, so long as it does not interfere with their daily duties. It is important to be extremely clear on what that means and how it will be enforced.

- **Ownership:** Employees may encounter issues on social media that they cannot solve on their own. It is important to understand whom to turn to in order to resolve any issues that employees may face. As discussed in the previous section, the go-to person is typically the social media manager, or social media "captain" for the company. Outlining the specific process behind this is critical, so each employee knows where to turn when the need arises.

- **Violations:** Outline the repercussions for employees that violate the policy. Be clear and concise, so that everyone understands the consequences of his or her actions.

IMPLEMENTING GUIDELINES

You may still be confused on the difference between policies and guidelines. To be clear, a social media policy is more comprehensive, specifically detailed, and is typically driven by legal requirements to reduce a company's risk in participating in social media.

Guidelines, on the other hand, are really more of a summary of behavioral expectations on the social web. A brief document will suffice to outline your set of engagement rules for the social web. As you build out your guidelines, here are some things to think about:

- **Social media objectives:** Let your employees know what the objectives are for social media within the company. Don't be afraid of being specific. For example, let the team know that social media is used as a (1) conduit for customer interactions and (2) a source for marketing inquiries. Providing a common goal will help unite your team around the overarching objective. Also, be sure to outline where the official company destinations are and the team who is responsible for managing them.

- **How to participate:** Begin by defining how you want your brand to be perceived on the social web. This is your social persona and it will drive how employees communicate and interact on the social web. Be as specific as possible here. Consider providing examples of what a conversation might look like. This would also include guidelines on how to address negativity from your audience.

- **With great power comes great responsibility:** Be sure that everyone understands that they are accountable for their actions on social media. Make sure everyone understands that they are working on behalf of the brand and that their interactions are a direct reflection of the company.

STRUCTURING THE GROUP, YOURSELF, AND THE COMPANY

Jeremiah Owyang and the Altimeter Group did significant research into how companies structure their approach to social media. According to Jeremiah, companies typically organize their social media in five ways.[3] Table 9.1 provides detail on each structure.

1. **Organic:** In this model anyone in the company can use social media in whatever way they choose. There is no predetermined organization. Jeremiah notes that ". . . the dots (representing those using social media tools) are inconsistent in size (frequency of use and involvement), and one set of employees are not directly connected to others."

2. **Centralized:** The company's social efforts are run by a centralized person or team, usually positioned in corporate communications. Most companies start here. "Notice that a central

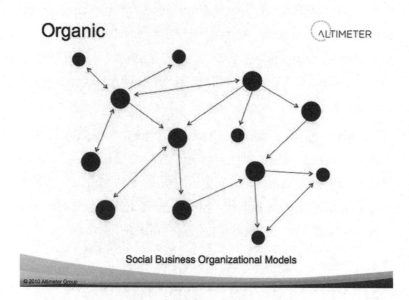

Social Business Organizational Models

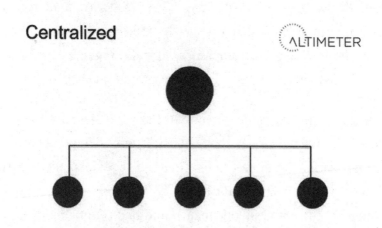

Social Business Organizational Models

group initiates and represents other business units, funneling up the social strategy to one group," says Owyang.

3. **Coordinated:** Here the company branches out from a centralized social-media unit. The central hub outlines corporate social policies and triages social efforts to the spokes, based on different roles. "Notice how a central group will help to provide an equal social media experience to other business units," says Owyang.

Social Business Organizational Models

4. **Dandelion or multiple hub-and-spoke:** This model is suited to large, international companies that are composed of multiple, distinct brands that act with a high degree of independence from the central organization. "Notice how each business unit may have semi-autonomy with an overarching tie back to a central group," says Owyang.

Multiple hub & spoke "Dandelion" ALTIMETER

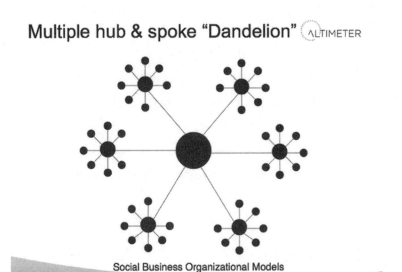

Social Business Organizational Models

© 2010 Altimeter Group

5. **Honeycomb or holistic:** The entire organization uses social media in an organized way. Social content in this model flows freely across teams and platforms. "Notice how each individual in the organization is socially enabled, yet in a consistent and well-ordered pattern," says Owyang.

Holistic "Honeycomb"   ALTIMETER

Social Business Organizational Models

© 2010 Altimeter Group

Table 9.1 Analysis: Pros and Cons of Each Social Business Model (Taken from Altimeter Group)

	Description	Advantages	Drawbacks	What no one tells you
Organic	Social efforts bubble up from the edges of the company, much like how Sun Microsystems encourages a blogging culture for all employees.	Looks authentic and is therefore trusted as multiple conversations appear closer to products and customers.	Risks an inconsistent experience to customers; one side of the company has no idea what the other side is doing; and encourages multiple enterprise software deployments. Later on this is a nightmare for IT data management and marketing.	This model is typical in large companies where control is difficult to enforce and occurs often in software-based companies. Mostly, I see companies transitioning out of this model.
Centralized	One department (usually corporate communications) controls all social efforts. See how Ford has deployed their efforts to engage in the tough discussions while staying on brand.	Great for consistent customer experience, coordinated resources, and rapid response times.	May appear very inauthentic as press releases are rehashed on blog posts or videos by less flexible executives.	Great for highly regulated industries or brands, yet make sure you bring forth the employee voices—not just faceless logos. Notice how Ford's Scott Monty is front and center.

(continued on next page)

Table 9.1   Analysis: Pros and Cons of Each Social Business Model (Taken from Altimeter Group) *(continued)*

	Description	Advantages	Drawbacks	What No one tells you
Coordinated	A cross-functional team sits in a centralized position and helps various nodes such as business units, product teams, or geographies maintain success through training, education, and support. See how the Red Cross keeps various chapters organized, especially during life-threatening crises.	The central group is aware of what each node is doing, maintaining a centralized pool of resources. This model provides a holistic experience to customers.	Costly. Executive support is required. Operates only with cross-departmental buy-in.	I see most companies headed toward this model, in order to provide safe autonomy to business units. **Tip:** The hub should act as an enabler—not as social police.

Multiple hub and spoke "dandelion"	Often seen in large multi-national companies where "companies within companies" act autonomously from each other under a common brand. Companies with multiple products like HP and IBM may naturally gravitate in this direction.	Business units are given individual freedom to deploy social media as they see fit, yet a common experience is shared amongst all units.	Requires constant communication from all teams to be coordinated, which can result in excessive internal noise. Requires considerable cultural and executive buy in, as well as dedicated staff.	Great for highly regulated industries or brands, yet make sure you bring forth the employee voices—not just faceless logos. Notice how Ford's Scott Monty is front and center.
Holistic "honeycomb"	Everyone is in customer service and support. Any employee who wants to be social is enabled. Dell and Zappos fit the bill.	The central group is aware of what each node is doing, maintaining a centralized pool of resources. This model provides a holistic experience to customers.	Costly. Executive support is required. Operates only with cross-departmental buy in.	I see most companies headed toward this model, in order to provide safe autonomy to business units. **Tip:** The hub should act as an enabler—not as social police.

Source: Owyang, Jeremiah, "Framework and Matrix: The Five Ways Companies Organize for Social Business," WebStrategy (blog), April 15, 2010.

Where does your current model lie, and where do you want to be? Jeremiah's advice is to "conduct an internal analysis of your company" to better understand where you stand and how you can improve your program. On his blog, he recommends following three steps to better understand how to make internal improvements:

1. **First, identify which organizational model you're in.** Companies should forward this post to the internal teams to have a discussion on which model they think they are in. What's interesting is that, most often, not everyone agrees. Rather than prescribing the current model, savvy executives should observe and see which model bubbles up from the ranks. The dialog that ensues afterwards is what you're really after.

2. **Next, discuss which model is your company's desired state.** Companies must evolve to respond to the social customer, yet their current state may be not be wholly evolved to meet this need. The decision of which model to aim for can't be made in a vacuum: The various business units, geographical locations, product teams, support, and service groups must be considered—this isn't about marketing alone. It's about restructuring your communications in order to put your customer's experience first.

3. **Recognize that this is more than an organizational chart: It's about cultural change.** Executives and their employees must realize the that social web is forcing companies to undergo a cultural change as customers connect directly to one another, often bypassing companies' input altogether. Your new structure and strategy will take time to develop. As a result, don't

expect these changes to happen quickly or without change-management programs.

As you begin to incorporate social media as part of the foundation of your marketing agenda, you will begin to see shifts in the way the group orients itself to the rest of the firm. Use these ideas and action steps to set an objective and usher in the kinds of changes you want to see to ensure your company's successful transition into a future of social media.

ACTIONS AND TAKEAWAYS

- Appoint a social media team from within your company. Recruit from departments whose expertise maps to the company's overall social media objectives.

- Organize areas of focus for your team, by industry, brand, competitor, or network.

- Establish a workflow that includes traceable systems of accountability and schedules that work to coordinate your team's efforts.

- Develop clear policies that outline legal considerations that your team needs to know before diving in.

- Develop guidelines to provide, from the outset, expectations about your team's engagement and voice.

CHAPTER 10

Stand Out by Measuring for ROI

Measuring return on investment (ROI) is a crucial part of every marketing program, heavily relied upon by executives as a measure of success. Intelligently discussing the ROI of social marketing with executives will allow them to see the tangible benefits it can provide.

It was initially difficult to pinpoint ROI measurement in social media, and in the course of figuring it out, ROI has been the subject of much debate. That said, it has matured significantly in recent years. Still, the ROI question gets a lot of attention from strategists attempting to measure the value and impact of social marketing.

Understanding and measuring ROI is the single most important topic for brands looking to differentiate their social-marketing strategies. The key to standing out in social media is knowing which metrics reflect your success and using this information to inform your overall social strategy. Brands that can demonstrate a return have an immediate leg up over competitors. It will illustrate where and why you can find repeatable success, as well as demonstrate the financial impact of your social-marketing investment.

This chapter will focus on the measurements that allow you to determine ROI. We will dive into the metrics that allow you to track conversions through social media, and how you can relate these metrics to your objectives.

TOP NINE METRICS TO TRACK SOCIAL-MARKETING ROI

If you are the one managing or implementing the social media–marketing strategy in your company, there's no doubt you've spent some time staring at certain numbers—followers, comments, influencers—trying to figure out what it all means. Marketers are challenged with identifying what is working well, what says "success," and how to make sense of multiple sources of disparate data.

Once you have your marketing strategy and goals in place, you need for the numbers you gather to tell you whether your strategy is on the right track. Most of you are already aware of several of these metrics, but my mission in this chapter is to help you understand how they affect ROI in the social space. These key indicators will explain how your social media program is faring from a reliable ROI perspective.

▌

Jeremiah Owyang, Web Strategist of the Altimeter Group, says that measurement should be the *number one priority*—in fact, he reports, the top priority for 48 percent of corporations was "creating ROI measurements" for internal programs. "Measurement can often help prove the efficacy of time, effort, and budget spent on certain social media tactics, and also gets you, as the social media marketer, to starting developing a formal measurement strategy and standards."[1]

A lot of social measurement guides start with the social-specific metrics. I list *conversions* first because that is how all other forms of marketing should be measured and social media should be no different. Conversions are THE metric, and all the measurements we look at after this are just ways of explaining the performance of the conversion metric.

1. CONVERSIONS

What is the ultimate goal of your marketing strategy—whether using social media or other channels? Conversions, of course! You want people to either become qualified leads that you can start selling to directly, or actual customers or clients who are ready to open their wallets for your brand by buying a subscription, using your Facebook application, or purchasing your product.

In order to show the long-term value of your program you'll need to show what all the other metrics mean in terms of conversions, since this is what ultimately provides value to your company.

Social Media Examiner (2010) gives a great rundown of how to measure conversions (www.socialmediaexaminer.com/8-social -media-metrics-you-should-be-measuring/).

If you've properly set up and configured your web analytics tool to measure social media referrals and you've defined your site goals, then you're ready to measure conversions. You should measure conversions from every social media channel and then roll this up into total conversions that can be attributed to social media.

You'll need to have a mechanism in place to know when a lead comes from social media. Most people use the combination of a URL shortener and some form of a "cookie" to attach a campaign to a lead. Some have integrated Google Analytics into their URL shorteners for a seamless transition to success metrics in analytics, while some companies are using proprietary shorteners and others are still trying to figure out how to do it.[2]

A key to accomplish tracking conversions comes with understanding how to develop unique, shortened URLs that embed specific codes that can track the lead back to its source. Paul Gillin discusses how to set up unique URLs on his blog:

> One thing you absolutely need to know, however, is how people reach your site. Unique URLs are a way to measure that. We're astonished at how many e-mails we still get from brand-name companies that don't make use of this simple tactic, which enables a marketer to specify a web address that is unique to the e-mail, tweet, wall post, or any other message. Unique URLs use a simple server redirect function to identify the source of an incoming click. They look like this: http://mycompany.23.com/public/?q=

ulink&fn = Link&ssid = 5155. Everything after the word "public/"
is a unique code that tells where the visitor came from.

Unique URLs enable your analytics software to track inbound
traffic from each source separately so you can determine the ROI
of each channel. Without unique URLs visits are simply classified
as "direct traffic," meaning that the source could be a forwarded
e-mail, bookmark, or an address typed into the browser.[3]

The code at the end of a link can be unique to the CRM and
web-analytics tool used, so be sure to check with your provider
before implementing them. With the codes in place you can use
tools such as Bit.ly to shorten the link to us in tweets, blog posts
or Facebook updates that point back to a conversion event (download, registration, purchase, etc.) and track the lead to its specific
source.

The ROI Connection: Converting social interactions into hard ROI
metrics is a simple way to judge the success or failure of social
media programs, but it is often overlooked by brands. Being disci-
plined about tracking links and offers back to the source is important, so you can gain more insight into how social media is driving
conversions.

2. REACH AND RELEVANCE

In social marketing, size does matter. You might hear the word
"reach" a lot in the social-marketing world, with some definitions
being clearer than others. For now, "reach" is how many people

your brand gets in front of. Another way of thinking about this is how many *opportunities* your brand has to spur action from potential customers or clients. The next step is obvious, based on this starting point: You're giving the opportunity to take action to those that are most interested in your brand by being there in the first place. The larger your reach, the more opportunities you have to reach.

I like to think of this as your "top of funnel" audience. This represents the audience with whom your brand will communicate regularly, through your social-marketing content. With that said, social reach is the total number of individuals that actively follow your company across all social platforms in which you engage. This metric is the basic count number of your fans, followers, and subscribers. To measure your company's social reach, you need to measure the total number of subscribers, fans, followers, etc. that you have accumulated across all of your social media platforms.

social reach = total number of fans, followers, and subscribers across all social media platforms

Next, use this initial social reach measure to determine your social reach velocity. Your social reach velocity is your ability to *grow* your social reach within social marketing over time:

social reach velocity = social reach growth month-over-month

For example, at the time of this writing, Awareness, Inc., had 27,603 Facebook fans, 9,273 Twitter followers, 1103 blog subscribers, 178 YouTube subscribers, and 8,942 Linkdin group subscribers, or a total social reach of 47,099. Two months earlier, the combined social reach of Awareness was 42,059. This represents a total social reach growth of 5,040, or a social velocity of 12 percent in two months.

Social reach velocity in this case was affected by significant growth in the numbers of Facebook fans and Twitter followers while blog subscribers and YouTube subscribers remained flat. Now (and this is where it starts to get exciting), here's how these metrics can inform strategy: To grow both social reach and social reach velocity, Awareness can focus on Facebook, which has the greatest reach return, while testing different approaches to engage and grow their following in the other social media platforms— Twitter, blog, LinkedIn, and YouTube. You can begin to see how this metric-based feedback spurs content creation and deployment creativity in your social media team, with sights set on affecting the numbers. For the purposes of this example I used our company's primary outposts. However, to truly understand our reach, I could have included other channels like Foursquare, Slideshare, Google+, or Pinterest, as well as individual employee accounts on Facebook, WordPress, YouTube, and blogs where Awareness is regularly syndicated (socialmediatoday.com, socialnomics.net, and business2community.com). This would have significantly increased the reach and velocity numbers, but makes the example presented here a bit more complex.

Note: *it's not just the size of your network that matters.* If your hottest commodity is wool socks and 80 percent of your 10,000 Facebook fans live in San Diego and Austin, TX, you might catch their attention for all of five days out of each year, if that. If your goal is to convert fans into purchasers, this is far from an ideal network breakdown of your social media impact. As you begin to look at the potential reach, as well as the potential effect, of your network there are a few things to focus on. First, aggregate numbers are useful things to review at a high level, but take the time to drill into those numbers to understand *who* makes up your audience.

- What is the demographic profile of your average fan (age, location, etc.)?
- What are the common themes they like to discuss?
- Are there commonalities in other "like's" "followers" or "friends"?
- Where do they like to interact most (which channels, types of content, etc.)?
- What percentage of these fans is "engaged" (participating actively in conversations)?
- Who are the most active members of the audience?

Of course you want the greatest possible potential. So sure, building a broad network with large reach can be a good thing. But in order for that potential to pay off somehow, you want to expend the effort growing both the size of your audience as well as the *density of its overall relevance* to your work. . . . So what we want isn't just reach, but *relevant reach*.[4]—Amber Naslund, 2010

Where to start and what to look at:

- Twitter followers or list inclusions. Spend time on sites like Twitter Analyzer (www.twitteranalyzer.com).

- Facebook fans or likes. View your Facebook Insights for detailed metrics.

- YouTube friends and subscribers. Take a look at your YouTube reports.

- Linkedin group members.

- Number of Foursquare check-ins. Be sure to own your venues to get this data.

- Number of internal community members and what they're saying.

- Blog or site RSS subscribers. Setting up your feed through Feedburner makes this easy.

- Solutions that collect and pull profile and demographic data together.

When possible, break down the numbers you gather by demographics, industry, interests. . . anything that helps get you closer to understanding how *relevant* these numbers are will ensure that your efforts aren't wasted.

The ROI Connection: The more people you touch and interact with, and the closer they are to your target profile, the more possibilities for sales you create.

3. INTERACTIONS

If the above metric is your *who*, the metric presented here is your *how*. It has to do with the engagement you generate with your audience, not just checking to see what people are saying. It focuses on how your network members are interacting with your social media presence from a quantitative and qualitative viewpoint. Are people consuming your content? Are they sharing it? Are they retweeting or replying to you on Twitter? Are they saying good things?

Your interactions metric is the total number of interactions on all of your content. To measure this metric you need to look at the number of shares, retweets, @replies, likes, comments, and favorites across all platforms.

interactions = the sum of interactions across all content
including shares, retweets, @replies, likes, comments, favorites

Next you will want to look at interaction trends over time. This is your interaction velocity. Through these data you can identify pieces of content that resonated most with your audience and get a clear idea about which content has the biggest effect on increasing your interactions.

interaction velocity =
interaction growth over time

Finally, you can reference the number of interactions you are generating by author, by content piece, and by theme, to gain deeper insight into what your most effective mechanisms are.

To understand which author is generating the best results look at your author interaction rate. This measures the average number of interactions per post by a specific author.

author interaction rate =

total number of interactions by author/

total number of posts by author

Your content interaction rate looks at the total number of interactions for a specific piece of content to identify which content is the most effective.

content interaction rate = total number of

interactions by individual post

Finally, your theme interaction rate is a little more complex. This requires tagging posts to all networks with specific themes and analyzing the interaction rates by themes. For example, if you were running an auto dealership, you may categorize posts into buckets like "Columbus Day Sales Promotions," "Vehicle Descriptions," "News and Events," etc. You would look at the total number of interactions in each category to gain deeper intelligence on which area generates the most engagement.

theme interaction rate = total number of interactions by theme/

total number of posts

Where to start and what to look at:

- Likes on Facebook.

- Views and shares on YouTube or Flickr.

- Tips on Foursquare.

- User-generated content across all channels.

- Twitter replies and retweets.

- Consumer sentiment within your own community.

The ROI Connection: The more your target audience is engaging with you online, the more you are relevant in their minds as a brand they enjoy. In this sense, interaction metrics are a good indicator of *brand loyalty*. The more loyal your social members, the more they'll promote your brand and purchase from you in the short and long terms.

4. ACTIVITY RATIO

You're always going to have some members—perhaps *most* members—of your social network who show little or no activity. By comparing the number of active members against the total number of members of your network and watching these trends over time, you'll be able to see what portion of your member base is active within your community. This is especially important when, for example, you launch a campaign to see whether there was a resulting spike in activity. It can inform you of how many network members you converted from being inactive participants to being active participants.

Start by looking at the total amount of interactions in comparison to your audience size.

activity ratio = amount of interactions/social reach

This will give you a sense of how active your audience is. That said, this metric can be somewhat deceiving, especially if a small percentage of your audience represents a majority of interactions. To better understand the activity of your audience, look at your active audience ratio or percentage of active members of your audience.

active audience ratio = number of active
audience members/social reach

You can also view this over a specified time period to understand the growth in the number of active members in your audience.

Where to start and what to look at:

- Facebook active fans versus non-active fans. Facebook Insights will show you this data.

- Number of RSS subscribers that open your blog posts, as viewed through Feedburner.

- Click-throughs on links posted to Twitter. You can measure this with most URL-shortening services, like bit.ly, or check your website analytics tools for traffic sources.

- Number of unique places your photos or videos are embedded.

The ROI Connection: Your network members want to get value from you, and they're more likely to engage with you when you give them something worth their while. If you're seeing more activity from your audience, it probably means you've given them something to *be active about*. The more value you provide, the more enthusiastic they'll be about your brand. Additionally, this is a good way to identify those members with the most consistent activity around your brand, allowing you to consider them as possible brand promoters.

5. CONTENT EFFECTIVENESS

There are three suggested content effectiveness measures that are also focused on ROI, which can help companies hone in on their content strategy. They are:

- **Comments-to-content ratio:** This measure allows companies to understand the effectiveness of their specific content campaigns. The more comments to a piece of content, the bigger the engagement. Jonas Nielsen, co-founder and managing partner of Mindjumpers, advises brands to "monitor activity and engagement rates—views and interactions such as posts, comments, and likes over time. To affect activity and engagement rates, continuously try new things, establish best practices, and piggyback on peers who are doing a great job."[5]

- **Comments-to-profile ratio:** This ratio measures a company's ability to engage with an individual over time. The more comments coming from a specific individual, the higher the likelihood that the brand will stay top-of-mind and then be considered when the customer is ready to buy. What to look at is how many comments are coming from specific individuals. It is a measure of both individual engagement and how engaging your content is to the individuals in your audience.

- **Content-to-share fatio:** This ratio gauges the ability of your content to travel beyond your social reach. The bigger the engagement, the higher the probability that your content will be shared within your audience's network, driving new prospects for your brand and products. Jeremiah Owyang, founding partner with Altimeter Group, advises, "Content that people are willing to register for is content that helps them make better decisions. If your content is good, you will see that, after a person consumes it, he or she is willing to share it, and make it spread."[6]

6. BRAND SENTIMENT

In order to make your social media program most effective, you've got to understand where your audience is engaged and what sentiments you're up against—not only at the beginning of the program, but on an ongoing basis. Categorize sentiment and watch for trends. On which channels is your audience congregating? Is your audience getting more positive over time? Are there problems or issues that are popping up regularly that should be addressed more strategically? Is your brand image getting better or worse?

As you monitor your brand, be sure to focus on two areas. First, look at which channels are the most active. Get an understanding of where your audience is and what they are talking about. Begin by getting a general feel of the overall sentiment within these channels before deciding on the types of content to publish regularly. Second, understand who is making the comments. Who are the most active participants and what are they talking about? What is their general sentiment?

Step back and think about a conversation you had in the last 30 minutes. How many *statements* in that conversation were unambiguously positive or negative. Not many, right? Getting a 20 percent sentiment mapping for individual comments is a very high number. On the other hand, think about the same conversation: Was the *overall sentiment* of the conversation positive or negative? That is far easier to cognitively classify. If businesses shift their focus to a conversation-based, rather than a comment-based, sentiment analysis, they will be able to get a far better read on the aggregate sentiment of online chatter.[7] —Mashable, 2011

Where to start and what to look at:

- Google Alerts for mentions of your brand and high-profile employees.
- Twitter searches for your brand and high-profile employees.
- Monitoring comments on your social media channels— Facebook, YouTube, your blog, or tips on Foursquare.
- Following inbound links back to the original sources to see what's being referenced and how.

- If you've got more resources available, there are more sophisticated social-media monitoring tools available that "can categorize online content, uncover linked concepts, and reveal the sentiment in a conversation as 'positive,' 'negative,' or 'neutral,' based on the words people use. The technology gets down to very specific elements and can separate positive and negative remarks within a single comment."[8] —KD Paine, 2010

The ROI Connection: The happier your audience is, the better customers they will be. Additionally, the more positive your overall brand sentiment is, the more positively new audience members will view your brand. In each case, there's a better chance they'll purchase from you when they need to make that decision.

7. INBOUND LINKS

The number of inbound links, or external sources that link back to one of your social media networks, is useful for two reasons:

1. In general, links offer more opportunities for people to find you while they're already looking at similar information. Not only do they offer another path for people to get to your content, but they also can create more qualified leads.

2. In the case of your website, inbound links give you a big SEO boost because they denote "authority" or signify—to Google at least—that someone out there likes your content.

If you're "looking for a magic number that automatically determines your social media prowess, you're not going to find it. Instead, the secret to tracking social media is tying together disparate data sources and selecting the metrics that make the most sense for your company. And those are never the obvious ones like Facebook fans and Twitter followers. Tracking social media may not always be easy and fast, but it's absolutely, 100 percent doable."[9] —Jay Baer at Convince and Convert, 2011

Where to start and what to look at

- Look harder at your traffic sources data on your web analytics tool. See who are your best referrers.

- Check out specific links from your social media properties that lead back to your website.

  - Bit.ly links

  - Blog links to a product page

  - Your logo on your YouTube page

- Try some of the following sites: Open Site Explorer (http://opensiteexplorer.org/) and SEOmoz (http://www.seomoz.com).

The ROI Connection: By creating more opportunities for people to come to you when they're looking for related online content and increasing your SEO through inbound links, you'll be presenting your brand to an audience that is more likely interested in your product or service. From a position of interest, they are more likely to make a purchase.

8. INFLUENCE

"Influence" is another one of those words: There are a lot of different definitions out there. Luckily, Brian Solis has come up with a concise definition that does the job: *Influence is the ability to cause desirable and measurable actions and outcomes.*[10]

Influence metrics show you what will happen when you interact within your social network, whether people will respond or take action in the ways you're hoping for.

In order to measure your own influence you'll need to lay out what are the goals of your social media program, so you know what you're shooting for (hence Brian's use of the word "desirable" in terms of outcomes). If you announce a new product upgrade on Facebook, do people rush out to get their hands on it? If you announce a discount at your restaurant on Foursquare, will people come eat with you? If you announce a ticketed event, how quickly will those tickets sell?

Where to start and what to look at

- Klout (link: http://klout.com)
- Twitalyzer (link: http://www.twitalyzer.com)
- PeerIndex (link: http://www.peerindex.net)

The ROI Connection: The more you can get people to act in beneficial ways in relation to your brand, the more proven success you have for your social-marketing program.

9. CUSTOMER SERVICE

Customer service has become much more important in a world where a single customer's voice can easily speak to millions. Gone are the days when problems were reported in private, on hotlines, or behind closed doors. Now they can be reported on Twitter, a blog, or on any number of social media platforms, right out in the open.

It's important that customer-service issues are handled well, and being timely can often make all the difference in the world. After all, we all know that having happy customers means either repeat customers or brand advocates—ideally both.

Customer service doesn't have to be just about addressing problems or concerns. It can also be linked to brand sentiment, which we talked about earlier. If customers are talking about you positively (or negatively) in a general way, the source of their sentiment can be related to customer-service issues, but not necessarily related to issues about your product.

Start by looking at the total number of inquiries handled through social media and track how issues are brought to a point of resolution on a monthly basis. You can also estimate a value per inquiry and use that to determine a cost-reduction ROI on using social channels to resolve traditional inquiries.

Where to start and what to look at

- Amount of time it takes to reply to someone on Twitter, especially if he or she is contacting you for product or service help.

- Number of customer questions that were answered positively on your Facebook page.

- Amount of positive mentions that your brand gets online.

- Number of shared how-to videos on your YouTube page.

- Number of customer complaints across channels and whether they were resolved. Watch this metric over time.

- Audience sentiment and engagement on specific issues.

Several of these metrics are qualitative in nature. Appropriate and specific measurements should be discussed with your team.

The ROI Connection: Having happy customers equals repeat business, brand loyalty, and brand advocates, all of which directly affect your sales.

▇

Interested in learning more mind-blowing stats? Head over to the blog and search for **3 Shocking Social Media Stats** that will amp up your marketing.

▇

WHY'S ALL THIS IMPORTANT AGAIN?

Because it all affects the bottom line. For instance:

- Your network could be generating sales leads.
- Your group could save the organization money by using social media for things like more cost-effective customer service.
- The level of brand awareness or brand loyalty could increase by engaging with your network members.
- You could position yourself as an industry leader by creating valuable content.

Whatever the direct benefits are, you need to be able to articulate the value of your social media program. No matter how enthusiastic you or your team are about your new strategy, you aren't going to get very far without some good, solid numbers!

Overall, it will be important to keep a few things in mind. As with any marketing activity, measuring social marketing is contextual and is tied to the specific goals for your organization. There are different levels of metrics associated with your industry, stage of social media maturity, and your role within the organization. Finally, social marketing can be effective in generating both long-term value as well as short-term measurable success.

Long-term value of social media

- Fostering and accelerating word of mouth—which helps increase brand awareness and preference over time.

- Building and fostering relationships—which fosters brand advocacy over time.

Short-term measurable success of social media

- Servicing customers directly—which can lead to lower customer-service costs over time.

- Lead generation and sales—which helps brands sell more effectively over time. For those companies focused on sales effectiveness, the major thrust of social marketing should be around filtering relevant social profiles and moving them through the social funnel into the traditional sales and marketing funnel. The end goal, of course, is the acquisition of new customers.

GOAL-BASED MARKETING EXAMPLES

Keeping this value framework in mind and integrating the advice and best practices from the best-in-class companies referenced in this chapter, I want to leave you with some clear-cut examples about how to tie these measurements together in conjunction with real goals. Let's take a look.

GOAL: NURTURE "SOCIAL LEADS" FROM THE SOCIAL FUNNEL INTO THE TRADITIONAL MARKETING FUNNEL

Proposed measurements:

- **Social reach-to-traditional lead ratio:** This ratio measures your ability to move social profiles into your traditional marketing funnel over time.

- **Social profile-to-sales ratio:** This indicator helps you track the number of social profiles turned into customers over time. Measure this ratio in the aggregate, as well as by individual social media platform—this analysis will help you hone in on which social media platforms generate the most return for your social media investment

GOAL: ACHIEVE "TOP-OF-MIND" AWARENESS IN THE BRAND CATEGORY

- Besides social reach and social reach velocity, as defined earlier, measure your share of social conversations. This is similar to traditional share of voice, but here share of social conversations measures your brand's ability to dominate social conversations. To measure this, monitor your brand mentions vis-à-vis all relevant conversations for a given period of time. Determine the set of keywords that best describe your area of social marketing focus and track the numbers of relevant conversations around this issue area versus the number of times your brand is explicitly mentioned within the same space.

$$\text{share of social conversations} =$$
$$\text{social brand mentions/all relevant conversations}$$

You can also assign monetary value to your share of social conversations. To do that simply use equivalent media value, measured as the cost for advertising on the platforms you are analyzing.

GOAL: MANAGE AND RESPOND TO SOCIAL BRAND CONVERSATIONS

Proposed measurements:

- **Brand reputation:** Comment sentiment is an important indicator of your brand's reputation in the social sphere (which, we can argue, is also becoming a useful echo chamber for how your brand's reputation fairs in the traditional world, based on your traditional marketing efforts as well). Monitor brand sentiment by social-profile type—customer, prospect, influencer—and assess how it changes over time. Increases in negative brand sentiment are a clear sign your brand reputation needs attention. Your ability to identify both positive and negative sentiment, and respond to it adequately in real time, will increasingly become a way to stay ahead of your competition.

- **Social profile churn:** Although most of your social marketing efforts are better spent on driving higher social profile engagement and social reach, watch your social profile churn rate—the rate at which you lose social profiles over time across your social media platforms. If your social profile churn rate is increasing, it is a warning sign—you may be over-promoting, too focused on your products versus the needs of your customers, or failing to adapt to the changes in the needs of your audience.

- **Customer satisfaction, retention and loyalty, reduced customer service costs:** Ultimately you're looking at your responsiveness to the social profiles that matter to you most—customer needs, prospect needs, influencer and media needs—all have an impact on the level of loyalty you can generate.

METRICS BY STAKEHOLDER

No matter what outcomes drive your social media marketing and investment, remember that social media marketing is not the same to all stakeholders. Jeremiah Owyang of Altimeter Group frames it best: "There are three different groups that need social media metrics: executives, business stakeholders, and those deploying and managing social media. At the top of the pyramid there's less data, less frequently, but at the bottom there's real-time data, and lots of it. Don't give engagement data to executives, as it doesn't measure the actual effect on business goals."[10] For special metrics by specific stakeholder group, refer to the Altimeter Group's ROI Pyramid.

Track and generate the metrics that are right for you and your program. Showing that the presence you establish on social media and the interactions you generate translate into meaningful business for your company will pave the way for your program's growth.

On the blog I added an infographic that talks about social marketing analytics and how to implement them. If you are looking for more details on social analytics, check it out.

The ROI Pyramid

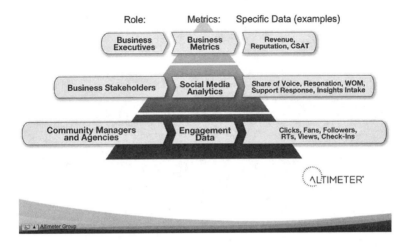

The ROI Pyramid

Role:	Metrics:	Specific Data (examples)
Business Executives	Business Metrics	Revenue, Reputation, CSAT
Business Stakeholders	Social Media Analytics	Share of Voice, Resonation, WOM, Support Response, Insights Intake
Community Managers and Agencies	Engagement Data	Clicks, Fans, Followers, RTs, Views, Check-Ins

ALTIMETER

Altimeter Group

ACTIONS AND TAKEAWAYS

- Understand conversion metrics and how it operates in social media. Know how people come to find you.

- Incorporate meaningful metrics into your program to track your impact.

- Use relative metrics between networks to adjust your strategy and extend your reach.

- Tie social media metrics into other companywide objectives to show executives how your team's efforts are benefiting the bottom line.

CHAPTER 11

Performing a Stand Out Social Marketing Audit

There are a lot of concepts and ideas presented in the previous chapters that you likely want to run out and implement immediately. Before you close the book, take the extra time and perform an audit on your current social marketing program. An audit will give you a concrete idea of where you are right now, so you can understand what needs to be improved.

AUDITING YOUR SOCIAL MARKETING

Companies of all sizes are scrutinizing their social marketing efforts to improve the return on their investment. Conducting objective social marketing assessments enables brands to stay focused, nimble, and relevant as they continue to move forward. Such audits also help savvy marketing teams identify areas of untapped opportunity for traction and growth. The process is organized into four steps:

1. Social reach and passion analysis
2. Digital conversations, volume, and trending-topic analysis
3. SEO health check
4. Developing your social-marketing effectiveness dashboard

Before you continue, please be advised that any objective assessment needs to be rooted in your organization's overall goals and objectives. Without the proper strategy lens, you and your team may end up investing in social strategies and executions that can take you off course. To start off on the right foot be sure to review Chapter 7 on content through Chapter 9 on management to learn how to keep the big picture in check as you proceed to build your social-marketing plan.

For the purposes of this audit, I used the airline industry as a case study to help illustrate a successful step-by-step audit as part of this book. Since I have used Delta as a case study in earlier chapters, we will focus on them as the subject of the study and audit. As we move forward through the four key steps, you'll see through Delta Airlines' experience how you too can perform a successful audit as you move forward with your social-marketing strategy. Please note that this is an independent and unbiased analysis of the space, using publically available information. I was not commissioned or paid by Delta, or any other airline, to develop this report. Also, for the report I used the primary social media presences for each company. Some airline carriers had multiple Twitter accounts, Facebook pages, etc. For the purposes of simplicity, I opted to use only the primary pages listed on their corporate websites. In your analysis, you would want to use aggregate numbers across all channels in which your company and competitors participate.

STEP ONE: SOCIAL REACH AND PASSION ANALYSIS

In this step you will be answering two key questions:

1. How big is your digital footprint—fans, followers, blog subscribers—compared to the footprint of your competitors?

2. What is the likelihood that your company, brand, or product is being discussed or that it will be discussed in the social realm?

One of the key rules of marketing dictates a simple fact: You are as big as your reach and as effective as your ability to touch your prospects and customers multiple times (also known as your marketing frequency). Social marketers seem to agree. In July 2011, Microsoft Advertising and Advertiser Perceptions surveyed social media marketers in six countries around the world. They found that 48 percent of social marketing budgets are geared toward new fan and follower acquisition on popular social networking platforms such as Facebook and Twitter. What the survey also found is that marketers value social platform presence more highly than advertising on these same platforms. For example, 74 percent of marketers thought it was very important to have a presence on Facebook, but only 57 percent felt the same way about advertising on Facebook.[1]

Let's start with some definitions:

- **Social footprint:** Your brand's presence on social platforms such as Facebook, Twitter, YouTube, blogs, Foursquare, etc. This is different from your *social reach*, which we discussed in Chapter 10. Social footprint also accounts for where your presence is established and how many people at your organization are participating internally.

- **Social frequency:** The number of times you engage with your social reach (your audience) via your social footprint.

- **Social amplification:** The number of times your social reach engages and shares with the content published through your social footprint. This is different from your activity ratio as discussed in Chapter 10, in that we are investigating the amplification of your content, not just the amount of activity it generates.

YOUR DIGITAL FOOTPRINT

An objective social-marketing effectiveness audit starts with measuring your social footprint against that of your top competitors. Such an audit will give you an indication of your position in the social domain relative to your competitors. For example, are you leading, doing the same, or faring worse than your competitors?

1. Start by researching your presence and the presence of your key competitors across all relevant social media platforms such

as Twitter, Facebook, LinkedIn, YouTube, Flickr, and blogs. Be sure to include any other channels on which you, or a competitor, hold a presence. This will help to identify destinations that you should consider joining. For example, one of your competitors may have developed a Pinterest page or may be doing a lot with Google+, yet no other competitors are there. This helps to identify possible locations to develop a useful presence.

2. Document the type of channels, number of channels, and total following within each channel for your brand and those of your competitors. The social footprint for Delta Airlines versus competitors is shown in Table 11.1.

   In terms of Social Reach, the clear leader is Southwest Airlines with 3,378,498 followers across platforms. Southwest is investing heavily in a cross-platform social-marketing strategy, actively participating in all key social platforms, and has the most dominant presence on Facebook. Although social reach is not a complete indication of your company's ability to participate and engage prospective users and customers in ongoing conversations, it is the first—and an important—piece of a brand's overall social-marketing effectiveness.

   Also of note is the use of video. Three players—Delta, American, and Southwest—are very heavy users of video in the web-content management space. All three have created impressive libraries of video content on YouTube. This is an area where Delta is the frontrunner and appears to have a slim advantage over the other participating airlines.

3. Create benchmarks for your own performance and that of your competitors on a monthly basis. You will be able to see at a

Table 11.1 Digital Footprint Analysis

Company	Facebook	Twitter	YouTube	Flickr	Blog	Social Reach
Southwest Airlines	2,099,639	1,274,266	4,593	Yes	Yes	3,378,498
JetBlue	576,222	1,670,782	1,126	Yes	Yes	2,248,130
American Airlines	269,225	341,205	5,013	Yes	No	615,443
Delta Airlines	298,853	304,341	7,350	Yes	Yes	610,544
US Airways	31,563	200,046	487	No	No	232,096

Please note: For the purposes of this analysis I did not include any Blog RSS subscribers or Forum participants. Also, for the purposes of simplicity, I focused on each airline's primary online destination. Some had multiple Twitter and Facebook accounts, but I elected to focus on the primary accounts listed on their website's homepage.

glance where your reach is stronger and where your team needs to invest in order to increase your foothold relative to your competition. In our example, Delta may want to further examine how to increase its footprint on Facebook and Twitter while ramping up its content creation and publishing capabilities.

SOCIAL FREQUENCY AND SOCIAL AMPLIFICATION

Next, measure your ability to drive conversations and engagement compared to that of your competitors.

1. You can use free social monitoring tools such as SocialMention. com (or paid listening tools such as Radian6).

2. Enter your brand name and jot down the results. To get more accurate results, use quotes around your brand name, for example, "Delta Airlines." This will avoid irrelevant results.

3. Focus on the following key measures. (Note: Socialmention. com measures your brand mentions as a percentage of total possible mentions within the last 24 hours. To conduct a deeper analysis of trends I recommend using a paid provider.)

   a. **Strength:** Measures the likelihood that your brand is being discussed in social media.

   b. **Reach:** As defined by social mention, is the number of unique authors referencing your brand, divided by the total number of comments. This is SocialMention's definition. I hesitate to include it for fear of anyone confusing it with the previous definition of social reach, but what this measure represents is a measure of influence. The higher the percentage, the more unique authors are commenting on your brand.

c. **Passion:** The likelihood that the individuals mentioning your brand would do so repeatedly.

d. **Sentiment:** A ratio of comments that are generally positive versus those that are generally negative.

Pay attention to the number of unique authors and the average time between mentions. This will help you identify supporters and influencers whom you may not be aware of.

4. Repeat these steps for your top competitors. Here's what our quick social amplification analysis revealed for Delta Airlines and its peer set (see Table 11.2).

Table 11.2 **Social Amplification**

KPI	American Airlines	Delta Airlines	JetBlue	Southwest Airlines	US Airways
Strength	29%	22%	16%	12%	13%
Reach	49%	37%	35%	40%	40%
Sentiment	4:1	4:1	14:1	5:1	4:1
Passion	34%	38%	45%	45%	27%

Source: Socialmention.com.

In this analysis, American Airlines takes the top spot, with higher overall reach and likelihood of the company being discussed across digital channels. However, it's clear that, in terms of sentiment, JetBlue is the winner. When people discuss the brand, chances are they are saying positive things about them. The 14:1 mark isn't just a high point for the airline industry, but outstanding for other industry segments as well. Also, both JetBlue and Southwest have a passionate group of advocates who repeatedly say good things about their brands.

A note of caution, when using tools such as Socialmention .com, you won't get fully representative or precise results. Use these indicators as directional points—as a quick diagnosis to gauge who tends to get more mentions, your brand or those of your competitors, and the likelihood of your brand or company being mentioned in the future. Treat these results as one piece of the bigger social-marketing effectiveness puzzle. If you see your brand in a less favorable position compared to your peers, make a note of that and focus your resources on investigating the drivers behind the numbers.

STEP TWO: DIGITAL CONVERSATIONS, VOLUME, AND TRENDING-TOPIC ANALYSIS

Assessing the volume and types of digital conversations helps you determine the size of the digital pie that you participate in. It shows you the frequency, type, and vibe of what matters to your customers, prospects, and opinion leaders. Assessing your inclusion in these conversations compared to that of your peers helps you gauge the effectiveness of your social-marketing efforts. It also helps you assess the level of additional effort and investment required for you to continuously participate and influence these conversations.

1. Start by defining your strategic keywords. To assess your ability to successfully market via social channels, you need to start by understanding the keywords that define your category and your product domain. Carefully selected keywords are the new digital currency: Get them right, and you are off to the races.

2. Finding the right keywords. Keywords are the expressions we use when we think about and search for what we need. Understanding what your prospects and customers already know about your category can give you an advantage when optimizing all of your marketing resources for maximum return—updating your website to match user search intent, building paid advertising campaigns to meet the specific demand of your users, or creating social content that hits home with your target audience. Here's how to determine what your keywords should be:

a. Develop a list of all the key category and product/service keywords that describe your category and product domain. For example, Delta is an airline carrier. Travel and leisure is its category domain. Delta's products are flights to national and international destinations. Its product domain keywords are "travel," "airline tickets," "flight," "cheap airfare," "discount airfare," "air travel deals to destinations worldwide," "book flights online," "airfares," and "book flights."

b. To find and select your keyword set, look for keywords that are:

- **Contextual:** Choose words that clearly describe your category in unambiguous ways.

- **Targeted:** Match the intent of your prospects. For example, "book cheap airline travel" may lure prospects looking to learn about Delta's flights.

- **Popular (but not too popular):** Check the popularity of your selected keywords to ensure the ones you are picking truly warrant your attention. Check to see if you are missing any important keywords. There are several tools to help you do that: Wordtracker, Wordstream, Google's AdWord Keyword Tool, and KeyWord Discovery.

For Table 11.3 I selected a set of keywords randomly, using Google's Adwords Ranking. In the analysis I investigated the global monthly search of the keyword, how competitive it is from an Adwords perspective, and where Delta ranks in terms of organic search results. Then I compared Delta's ranking to American Airlines. Overall, Delta's presence is very strong, with several keywords ranking in the top ten results. In addition, Delta has multiple keywords for which they rank higher than American.

Note: For your analysis you would likely use all competitors. For the purposes of simplicity I used only Delta and American.

This type of analysis gives you the ability not only to benchmark where you are today, it also allows you to focus on specific terms that help improve your conversions, relative to the competition.

Selecting your keywords is both an art and a science. Choose wisely, and you will see an increase in traffic, higher interest in your products, and more sales. Once you know your keywords, continue by measuring the digital chatter associated with them. The higher the volume of conversations, the more you may need to invest to stay top-of-mind and drive prospects

Table 11.3 Keyword Analysis

Keyword	Global monthly search	Competition	Delta.com rank (Google)	AA.com rank (Google)
airline tickets	5,000,000	94%	8	15
airline ticket	3,500,000	94%	11	16
air lines	20,400,000	27%	1	16
airline fares	2,740,000	95%	25	14
plane fares	2,240,000	98%	36	n/a
airline fare	3,350,000	96%	17	13
plane fare	1,830,000	98%	41	34
air lines tickets	74,000	85%	7	12
cheapest airline tickets	1,500,000	98%	50	n/a
air line tickets	110,000	94%	6	12
fly tickets	2,740,000	88%	8	20
airlines fares	368,000	84%	8	12
airline	83,100,000	31%	5	16
cheap air fare	1,220,000	99%	n/a	21
cheap airlines	6,120,000	100%	22	43
air fares	3,350,000	95%	10	12

discount airline tickets	110,000	98%	17	41
cheap airline tickets	1,830,000	98%	n/a	n/a
airlines tickets	2,740,000	90%	6	12
cheap airfare	9,140,000	99%	38	n/a
air line ticket	110,000	93%	8	13
flight deals	550,000	99%	43	38
air line fares	49,500	90%	27	37
discount airfare	246,000	97%	22	44
cheap air fares	1,000,000	98%	49	n/a
cheap airlines tickets	1,500,000	98%	n/a	46
discount flights	301,000	96%	29	35
air tickets	5,000,000	95%	16	20
airlines	83,000,000	28%	9	6

Source: Google Adwords, SEOMoz.

and customers to your web properties. Our suggested next step helps you do just that.

3. Use your strategic set of keywords to measure digital conversations. The key questions you will be answering in this stage are:

a. How vibrant is the digital dialog about your category?

b. How many conversations happen, and where do these happen?

c. What is your digital share of voice relative to your competitors?

A few key clarifying points and definitions:

- Most listening tools have limitations, such as allowing you to go only 30 days back in time. This puts you at risk of examining a period of time that is not wholly representative (for example, when there is a relative lull in your industry). Use your findings as benchmarks and revisit the statistics monthly to see if there are any major fluctuations in the volume of conversations, types of conversations, or the channels where these conversations occur.

- Digital conversations, these are all mentions of your selected keywords across publicly open digital destinations, such as social networks, blogs, forums, and mainstream media sites.

- Digital share of voice, this is an estimated share of brand mentions for a select keyword set compared to that of its select competitors.

VIBRANCY OF DIGITAL CONVERSATIONS/DIGITAL SHARE OF VOICE

There were more than 2,900 digital conversations across platforms that included Delta and their competition, according to SocialMention.com. Close to 23 percent of those were driven by Southwest Airlines mentions, followed by 21 percent that were mentions for American Airlines. Delta was mentioned in just over 18 percent of all conversations.

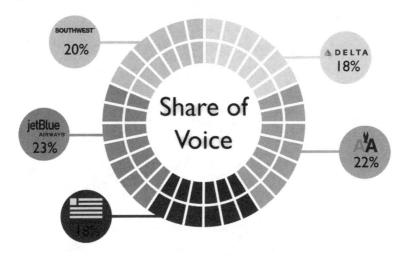

CALCULATING SHARE OF VOICE

There are several tools, such as Sysomos, Radian6, and Socialmention.com, that can help you calculate share of voice. For the purposes of this example, I used Socialmention to help demonstrate that even free tools can produce valuable results.

Blogger Ron Jones provides an excellent step-by-step process for calculating share of voice, which I will summarize below.

Please note that this is the method I used to calculate share of voice in the Delta example.

Go to Social Mention and type in your company name in quotes ("organization name") and click "search." Make sure you select "all" in the pull-down menu next to the search box. This will make sure you are using only exact, relevant matches.

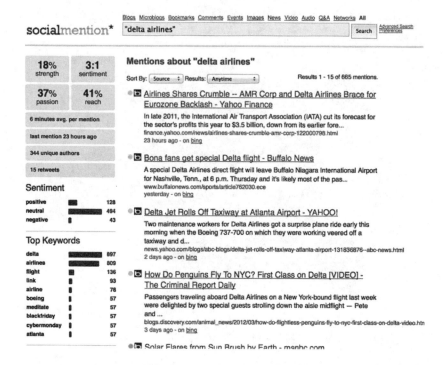

On the results page, you can see the total number of mentions at the top right, as you can see in Table 11.4 (in our case, Delta has 533 mentions). You can adjust the date range to suit your needs. You should scan through the mentions to get a feel for what is being said and by whom. This will help you put the mentions in proper context.

Table 11.4 **Share of Voice Analysis**

Brand	Total mentions	Share of voice
American Airlines	533	18.10%
Delta Airlines	639	21.71%
JetBlue	519	17.63%
Southwest Airlines	672	22.83%
US Airways	581	19.74%
TOTAL	2,944	100.00%

Now go over to the chart on the left and look at the ""senti-ment" panel. You will see positive, neutral, and negative sentiment figures. If you add these up, it will equal the total mentions.

Open up a spreadsheet and type in each of these numbers. Now, do a search on each of your competitors you are tracking and record the same numbers in the spreadsheet.

To calculate the share of voice, you need to add up the mentions for each company and divide by the total number of mentions. For Delta you would divide 533 by 2,944 to get 18.1 percent. This is the online share of voice for Delta. Here is the general formula:

$$\text{(positive mentions)} + \text{(neutral mentions)} / \text{(total mentions for all companies)}^2$$

Please note that I modified Ron Jones's example to fit our case study.

The final step in your objective audit of your social-marketing effectiveness is focused on your company's ability to rank high in organic search results.

STEP THREE: SEO HEALTH CHECK

Search is the second most popular activity online. It is likely that your prospects and customers use search to find out about new products, services, and solutions to suit their needs. Your ability to be found—and be ranked on the first page of search-engine results for these targeted searches—is key to your company's ability to grow its following and get more people engaged.

Here are the steps for conducting a quick search engine optimization (SEO) health check:

1. Use SEO assessment tools to get the insights you need:

   a. **Free tools:** HubSpot's marketing grader is a great way to get started.

   b. **Paid tools:** SEOMoz is among the best SEO health check tools currently available.

2. Important metrics to include in your SEO health check:

   a. **Your overall marketing grade:** Digital Marketing effectiveness grade via HubSpot.

   b. **Linking domains:** the number of unique sites linking back to your website.

   c. **MozRANK:** SEOmoz's general, logarithmically scaled ten-point measure of a website's global link authority or popularity

   d. **Klout score:** Social Media influence score. It analyzes your reach, influence, and the power of your network.

   e. **Unique visitors:** Measured from Compete.com. Looks at the number of unique visitors to your site on a monthly basis.

Table 11.5 **SEO Assessment**

	Delta Airlines	American Airlines	JetBlue	Southwest Airlines	US Airways
Overall grade	91	70	90	75	69
Linking domains	36,265	32,804	12,969	24,943	20,552
MOZ rank	7	7	8	7	6
Klout score	71	69	69	74	60
Unique visitors	6.240,656	5,584,711	3,843,833	10,435,935	2,797,452

The quick analysis in Table 11.5 shows that Delta is doing very well overall compared to its competitors. They are on par with the best-in-class companies within its peer set and are leading in several areas.

STEP FOUR: DEVELOPING YOUR SOCIAL-MARKETING EFFECTIVENESS DASHBOARD

Developing a social-marketing effectiveness dashboard will help you benchmark and track your progress and continuously identify opportunities for growth. Moreover, the dashboard will provide you with an objective way of measuring your social-marketing effectiveness so you minimize wasted effort and get the most return for your social-marketing investment. Customize your dashboard to meet your needs and business objectives, then treat your dashboard as the proven way to diagnose issues and discover areas for improvement. Update it monthly, so you can quickly diagnose both issues that require your team's attention and new opportunities for growth. For example, based on our quick analysis in Steps 1 through 3, we would suggest that Delta track the key areas represented in Table 11.6 on a monthly basis.

INCREASING SOCIAL REACH

1. Build presence anywhere it matters—across all relevant platforms. Best-in-class brands have an established presence across multiple social platforms. Earlier this year, Awareness examined top-performing brands in terms of greatest social reach and follower engagement, using the Awareness social media management platform. We found that companies using the Awareness social media management platform have at least 13 Facebook Fan pages and ten or more Twitter profiles.[3]

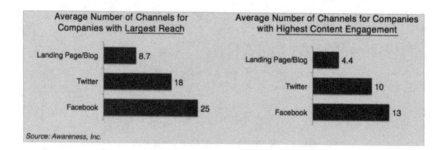

2. Optimize your social presence for popular search terms. Make sure that your profile and company descriptions across all your digital properties include your strategic keyword terms, carry a consistent look, and convey the same message.

3. Update all of your digital properties with your social platform icons.

Table 11.6 Social Marketing Dashboard

	Delta Airlines	American Airlines	JetBlue	Southwest Airlines	US Airways
Digital footprint grid					
Facebook	298,853	269,225	576,222	2,099,639	31,563
Twitter	304,431	341,205	1,670,782	1,274,266	200,046
YouTube	7,350	5,013	1,126	4,593	487
Blog	Yes	No	Yes	Yes	No
Social search	610,544	615,443	2,248,130	3,378,498	232,096
Social amplification					
Strength	22%	29%	16%	12%	13%
Reach	37%	49%	35%	40%	40%
Sentiment	4:1	4:1	14:1	5:1	4:1
Passion	38%	34%	45%	45%	27%
Delta versus competitors SEO assessment					
Overall grade	91	70	90	75	69
Linking domains	36,265	32,804	12,969	24,943	20,552
MOZ rank	7	7	8	7	6
Klout score	71	69	69	74	60
Unique visitors	6,240,656	5,584,471	3,843,833	10,435,935	2,795,452

4. Monitor for keyword mentions across platforms in real time. You can use free tools, such as Kurrently.com, which captures Twitter and Facebook open posts, or an advanced Twitter search, if your digital conversations are driven by this platform.

INCREASING SOCIAL STRENGTH AND PASSION

1. Bank on popular keywords. Develop targeted content that you can publish across all your key social media platforms where you have presence.

2. Identify and follow influencers across platforms. Opinion leaders have the power to amplify your messages across platforms and help you increase your social reach, passion, and amplification. Here are a few ways to identify influencers:

   a. Use the Twitter "Similar to Profile" function. Once you identify new influencers to follow, then find and engage with them on all relevant platforms (their blogs, Facebook pages and LinkedIn profiles).

   b. Use free tools, such as Klout.com and Twellow.com. You can search by name or by keyword.

   c. Paid tools, such as Traackr and SocMetrics let you identify top influencers by topic or subject areas. Again, this is where your top domain keywords would come in handy.

3. Know when to publish for maximum effect. As you continue to grow your reach, you will be publishing more content that is targeted to the needs of your users. Maximize your efforts by publishing at times when your posts will have the most impact. According to a recent infographic by AddThis, reviewed by

Jennifer Van Grove from Mashable,[4] most people share around 9:30 a.m. on Wednesdays. Expect that 75 percent of the clicks will happen within two minutes of your publishing.

Interested in seeing the complete infographic? Head over to the blog and search for **AddThis**.

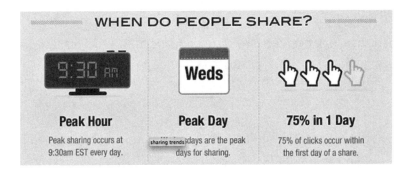

MEASURE AND ADAPT

Update your social-marketing effectiveness dashboard monthly. Continue to diagnose issues and identify opportunities to improve your social-marketing effectiveness. The social realm is very iterative and dynamic. Your social-marketing strategy should be too. Use this guide to gauge the effectiveness of your social-marketing efforts as you move forward. Update your social-marketing effectiveness dashboard monthly to stay on top of your industry and competitors and to implement new best practices. The added benefit of your social-marketing effectiveness dashboard is that you will always have your key social performance indicators at your fingertips. This way you can always be able to answer the questions: *How well are we doing with social?* and *What can we do better?* for your senior executives.

I posted a great infographic that visually represents how to deliver a social audit on the blog. Head over and check it out.

ACTIONS AND TAKEAWAYS

- Perform a comprehensive audit to get a solid idea of where you stand in social media.
- Trace your digital footprint, social frequency, and social amplification relative to your specific competitors.

- Determine the percentage of the trend-based conversations that are taking place all the time online that you are a part of.

- Don't forget about SEO (search engine optimization). Search is the most popular activity online, so make sure your initiatives improve your ability to be found through basic search.

CHAPTER 12

Out Standing!

STANDING OUT IS A CHOICE

First off, thanks for sticking with me through the book and for making it this far! When I discuss the content of the book, I typically get two distinct reactions. The first is excitement. The individuals that fall in this category get the concepts, understand the value of the book, and want to jump in and start implementing. Many of you likely fall in this bucket and are psyched to put the book down and start working. If that describes you—awesome!

The other reaction I see is bemusement. These people love the concepts and approach, but often view them as too complex, costly, or time consuming. If you fall into this bucket, I hear you, and the good news is that you are not alone. Every individual and company featured in this book had one thing in common: When first embarking on a social-marketing strategy they crawled before they ran. Everyone who has established a robust strategy has implemented processes, campaigns, and tactics one at time and learned from their mistakes along the way. In other words, it didn't happen overnight; they grew into developing stand out social-marketing strategies.

The information in this book can be implemented in phases. I expect that some of you had already implemented a few of the concepts before reading the book, while others may still be at the starting line. It's okay to implement some of the ideas and leave others behind to return to at a later date. It all depends on where you and your business are in the process. The biggest thing you should leave with is the motivation and belief that your social marketing can stand out.

In the introduction of this book I encouraged you to take the red pill. Like Neo in *The Matrix*, marketers are at a crossroads and face a big decision. Choose the red pill and stand out, or take the blue pill and continuing operating in a world of marketing sameness.

Those taking the red pill will find more opportunities as they are speaking to consumers in the manner that today's consumers prefer. These marketers choose to participate in the revolution and work to define standards, metrics, and the landscape of the social media universe. Those opting for the blue pill will be left to sit back as the world changes without them. *The decision is yours.*

THE FUTURE OF SOCIAL MARKETING

A common question I get is "What's next for social marketing?" Last year, Awareness released the "State of Social Marketing" annual report, featuring the Top Areas For Social Marketing Investment and Biggest Social Marketing Challenges. The findings and insights contained in this report are revealing on several levels and echo some of the key takeaways of this book.

SOCIAL MARKETING MATURITY

Social marketing is entering a stage of increased maturity, and with it, savvy, socially oriented businesses are starting to embrace social media as part of their company's DNA. This transition comes with an understanding that siloed approaches to social marketing are not effective, and scaling social marketing requires the adoption of new organizational structures, processes, and technological infrastructures that can help the enterprise optimize on a consistent basis. Under way is a shift that will lead marketing teams to focus on active social media management for increased lead generation and sales.

This is important for stand out strategists to understand. It's no longer about whether to participate in social media or not, it's about *how* you participate. Increasingly, businesses that adopt social marketing are shifting their focus to social media's effect on bottom-line performance. To truly stand out, it's up to you to build your social marketing on that foundation. You have the opportunity to do this by paying attention to the right conversations and driving a social strategy that focuses on the bottom line.

C-LEVEL INVOLVEMENT WITH SOCIAL MARKETING

Top-of-mind for executives and senior managers is ROI, integration of social media with lead generation and sales, and expansion of social presence and reach. It is clear that the C-level wants more proof before they allocate additional organizational resources to social marketing. This is why only 8 percent of the respondents in the Awareness report stated 2011 social-marketing budgets of over $50,000 per year, with only 12 percent of the organizations reporting teams of more than five social marketers. For those organizations that fall in the other 92 percent or 88 percent, the executives need to realize that, in order to give their social-marketing initiatives a chance, they need to invest in the effort.

In the future, we will see a resolution to the cost-benefit conundrum. Executives will start to adopt new processes and technologies that will not only help them scale the effort, but get the data that clearly links to ROI.

THE RIGHT SOCIAL-MARKETING INFRASTRUCTURE

Social marketing maturity will continue to increase, as companies continue to adopt new processes and technologies that will help scale their initiatives. Savvy social businesses are moving beyond the "let's allocate resources of a few people to social" mentality and are incorporating robust social media management platforms. These platforms will provide the ability to pay attention to and analyze social conversations, while creating effective response and content mechanisms to increase customer engagement and, ultimately, sales. Our industry is reaching this maturity tipping point— 78 percent of marketers report monitoring social media channels for mentions of their brand at least a few times a week, while 62 percent reported monitoring industry conversations with the same frequency. Nineteen percent of surveyed marketers reported using a social media management platform, and these are the leaders who will be reaping the most benefit from their efforts.

In the future, we will see marketers moving beyond brand-focused monitoring, to monitoring behaviors and conversations that represent a likelihood of generating sales. While the transition in this area will be slow in most companies, the ones that capitalize on it first will generate significant advantages over competitors who wait.

SOCIAL MEDIA PLATFORM USE IS GROWING

Experienced social marketers report that they plan increased usage of social marketing platforms beyond the Big Three (Facebook, Twitter, and LinkedIn) to include: blogs (91 percent) YouTube (86 percent), Foursquare (59 percent), SlideShare (43 percent), Flickr (50 percent), and Tumblr (30 percent). Driven by increasingly fragmented user consumption habits, companies clearly see the need to have an expanded social presence that will allow them to follow and engage their prospects and customers on multiple channels and networks. This proliferation of channels and the corresponding need to successfully engage in all of them will make the job of social marketers increasingly more complex. This, in turn, will necessitate the adoption of robust tools to manage presence, monitor and report on activity, and tie efforts to the organizational bottom line.

This past year, platforms like Google+, Pinterest, Path, and others burst onto the scene and gained significant subscribers, leaving brands to question whether or not they should be participating. Stand out companies adopt as early as possible and help define the end-user experience.

WHAT NEXT?

Lots of information was presented in this book. I bubbled up the steps to help you quickly implement what you have learned.

- **Start with Chapter 11:** You may think this recommendation flies in the face of the natural order of this book, and you would be correct. I opted to include the *social marketing audit* in Chapter 11 at the end of the book because, from the pages that preceded it, you gained the insight and knowledge you need to understand why you were conducting the audit. You gained the ability to identify what it means to stand out, and gained an understanding of which areas to focus on. In practice, however, it makes sense to start with the audit.

  The audit will allow you to benchmark where you are and will allow you to use that knowledge to identify the areas where improvement is needed. Follow the example of the airline industry, and generate your own data to gain a deep understanding of where you stand in relation to your competitors. This will lay the foundation for your future path in social media, and provide a detailed outlook on where your attention is best placed.

- **Pay attention!** Listening to the social web for mentions of your brand should be a component of your social-marketing strategy. However, it's more important to tie that listening to bottom-line results. While it helps to know industry trends and who is speaking about your brand, the real art and science of paying attention is about focusing on the conversations that demonstrate a likelihood of generating revenue. Following the guidelines presented in Chapters 3 and 4 will help you pay attention and identify sales conversions immediately.

- **Stimulate interaction:** For your social marketing to stand out you can't rely on a "build it and they will come" approach. To stand out you need to stimulate interactions from the audience. Build it and then invite people to participate in the game with you. Develop unique and interactive campaigns that encourage interactions. Use the examples and steps presented in Chapters 5 and 6 to increase your interaction rates within your audience.

- **Compelling content:** A stand out social marketing program is built on content. The content you provide to your audience is what will drive repeat and loyal visitors, as well as increase sales conversions. While I only provided one chapter on content in this book, there are excellent books that dig much more deeply into content marketing. The two books I highly recommend are *Content Rules* by C.C. Chapman and Ann Handley and *Get Content, Get Customers* by Joe Pulizzi. If you are looking for a deeper dive into content marketing, pick up both books; you won't be disappointed.

Want to learn more about content? Visit the blog and search for Social Content for a recent post titled "Social Marketing: It's (still) all about the content."

- **What your audience doesn't see is just as important as what they do see:** Too many brands jump into social marketing without considering the back-end processes that will make or break your success. Without the proper processes in place it's impossible to have a stand out strategy. Consider the workflows and processes behind the scenes that will help define your social strategy. Follow the instructions in Chapter 9 to make sure you have the right policies and procedures in place.

- **Measure the right stuff:** When I first started at Awareness, I was excited to go to my first board of directors meeting to outline the progress we had made in social media. In less than three months, we had tripled our Twitter following and built a solid presence on Facebook and LinkedIn. After presenting the impressive growth stats, the chairman politely asked: *This is great, but can you tell us how this is translating to sales?* Doh! I made it my mission to answer that question, and by the next meeting I was able to granularly explain how social media had affected our sales pipeline growth and which deals were sourced through social channels. This allowed me to apply a very specific ROI to what we were doing.

  The key is focusing on measuring the right things. While views and engagement metrics may look great, challenge yourself, and your company, to focus on those metrics that demonstrate bottom-line effects. This will help you demonstrate value in social media and showcase ROI.

LET'S KEEP CHATTING!

As I mentioned early on, I want to connect with you! Having a better picture of the specific challenges *you* face and *your* business objectives, I am better able to serve you through the information I provide. To that end there are a bunch of ways for you to reach out and connect with me directly. If you need clarification as you read through the book, if you want to ask questions, if you need advice, ANYTHING—please reach out using any of the mechanisms below:

E-mail: mike@standoutsocialmarketing.com

Twitter: @bostonmike

Facebook: http://facebook.com/bostonmike

Facebook page: http://facebook.com/standoutsocial

LinkedIn: http://www.linkedin.com/in/lewismich

Blog and website: http://www.standoutsocialmarketing.com

On www.standoutsocialmarketing.com you will find a vast number of resources that will extend the concepts presented in this book. Integrated into that site you will find:

- **Stand out strategies:** Case studies featuring brands with a differentiated approach to social media.

- **Stand out strategists:** The individuals who have implemented stand out strategies within their business.

- **Stand out infographics:** A database of infographics featuring the latest and greatest details on the changing landscape of social media.

- **Stand out blog:** A collection of blog posts featuring some of the greatest thinkers in the social media space.

BE OUTSTANDING!

Some people in your organization may still believe in "old-school" marketing and tell you that social media is a fad that will pass. In this book you have come to see that it's possible to have a stand out social marketing strategy. It doesn't matter what industry you are in or what resources you have to execute social marketing. You have the ability to develop an outstanding presence and make an impact.

You have the tools, knowledge, case studies, and resources to make it happen. So, what are you waiting for? *Be Outstanding!*

Afterword:
In It for
the Long Haul!

You want to invest in the future success of your company. You want to do what you can to ensure growth. So, what does social media have to do with this? Everything.

Life is complex; those that simplify it win. We must do the same when it comes to social media, simplify. First and foremost, it's about people. Second, it takes time to foster these relationships both online and offline. Those that do will reap the rewards today and in the digital decades ahead.

Every company will claim that their best customers come from word of mouth: customers telling customers or C2C. Social media brings this C2C in a scalable format and in a way where companies can participate in the conversation. What company wouldn't want to participate in word of mouth on digital steroids? It's also now world of mouth.

The hurdles for social media are plenty: What are the metrics? ROI? Who posts? Who owns the customer or client? And what to say?

Granted there is no easy formula. This stuff isn't easy. *That's why it's so great.* The reason it's great is that when stuff's hard, not a lot of people want to do it, let alone do it *well*. It's a way for you to stand out and beat your competition. Mike has put a tremendous amount of effort into breaking down, helping you visualize how to build your social media strategy from the ground up, or how to reassess what you already have working for you. Take these tips, work to implement these ideas, and look around to learn from who's tried what.

There is a lot of success waiting to happen out there on the social web, and those that do it well, with focus and long-term vision, will see results today and in the digital decades ahead.

Erik Qualman
International Bestselling Author of
Socialnomics and *Digital Leader*

Notes

CHAPTER 1

1. From Wikipedia, http://en.wikipedia.org/wiki/Product_ differentiation.
2. Mutyala, Sridhar, "Positioning and the Principle of Minimum Differentiation," Eight Leaves Blog January 12, 2011. http://www .eightleavesmedia.com/2011/01/positioning-and-the-principle-of -minimum-differentiation/.
3. Heine, Christopher, "Levi's 'Likes' Facebook a Whole Lot, Launches 'Friends Store' on Jeans Site," ClickZ.com, April 28, 2010. http:// www.clickz.com/clickz/news/1710543/levis-likes-facebook-whole -lot-launches-friends-store-jeans-site.
4. Source: Owyang, Jeremiah "List of Social Media Management Systems," Web-Strategist.com, March 19, 2010. http://www.web -strategist.com/blog/2010/03/19/list-of-social-media-management -systems-smms/.

CHAPTER 2

1. Quinton, Brian, "How to Find Sales Leads on Social Media," Entrepreneur.com, January 25, 2011. http://www.entrepreneur.com/ article/217901.
2. "The Social Funnel: Driving Business Value with Social Marketing," Awareness, Inc., July 27, 2011. http://info.awarenessnetworks.com/ Social-Funnel.html.

3. Gilbert, Alorie, "Salesforce Users Suffer More Downtime," ZDNet, February 1, 2006. http://www.zdnet.co.uk/news/networking/2006/02/01/salesforce-users-suffer-more-downtime-39250119/.

CHAPTER 3

1. Milletti, Umberto, "Social Selling Throughout the B2B Sales Cycle," Social Media B2B (blog), January 3, 2011. http://socialmediab2b .com/2011/01/b2b-social-selling/.
2. Fredrickson, Clark "Case Study: How IBM Uncovers 'Millions of Dollars' Worth of Sales Leads with Social Media," eMarketer.com, April 30, 2010 http://www.emarketer.com/blog/index.php/case -study-ibm-drives-millions-dollars-worth-sales-leads-social-media/.

CHAPTER 4

1. Rao, Leena, "Gartner: Social CRM Market Will Reach $1B In Revenue by 2012," TechCrunch.com (Blog), August 30, 2011. http:// techcrunch.com/2011/08/30/gartner-social-crm-market-will-reach -1b-in-revenue-by-2012/.

CHAPTER 5

1. Solis, Brian, "The Rules of Smarter Engagement," BrianSolis.com (blog), November 9, 2011. http://www.briansolis.com/2011/11/ the-rules-of-smarter-engagement/.
2. Solis, Brian, "The Rules of Smarter Engagement," BrianSolis.com (blog), November 9, 2011. http://www.briansolis.com/2011/11/ the-rules-of-smarter-engagement/.

CHAPTER 6

1. CSP Daily News, "Mars Distributing Random Acts of Chocolate," September 19, 2011. http://www.cspnet.com/news/ snacks-and-candy/articles/mars-distributing-random-acts-chocolate.
2. Beirut, "USA Today's #America Wants Twitter Campaign – Learn Social Media by Example," ThoughtPick (blog) May 21, 2010. http://blog.thoughtpick.com/2010/05/usa-todays-americawants -twitter-campaign-learn-social-media-by-example.html.
3. Prime Infographics, July 19, 2011. http://primeinfographics.com/ 2011/07/65-of-all-people-are-visual-learners/.

CHAPTER 7

1. Taken from the Awareness e-book *The Social Marketing Funnel* 2011 http://info.awarenessnetworks.com/Social-Funnel.html.
2. Taken from the Awareness e-book *The Social Marketing Funnel* 2011 http://info.awarenessnetworks.com/Social-Funnel.html.
3. Brogan, Chris, "How Outposts Improve Your Ecosystem," ChrisBrogan.com (blog), January 9, 2010. www.chrisbrogan.com/how-outposts-improve-your-ecosystem/.
4. Brogan, Chris, "How Outposts Improve Your Ecosystem," ChrisBrogan.com (blog), January 9, 2010. www.chrisbrogan.com/how-outposts-improve-your-ecosystem/.
5. Taken from the Awareness e-book *The Social Marketing Funnel* 2011. http://info.awarenessnetworks.com/Social-Funnel.html.
6. Taken from the Awareness e-book *The Social Marketing Funnel* 2011. http://info.awarenessnetworks.com/Social-Funnel.html.
7. eMarketer.com Interview, "Marketo Gets Creative with B2B Content Marketing," September 20, 2011. http://www.emarketer.com/Mobile/Article.aspx?R=1008618.
8. Scott, David, "Content Curation," WebInkNow.com (blog), February 23, 2011. http://www.webinknow.com/2011/02/content-curation.html.
9. Social Media Examiner, 2011 Social Media Marketing Industry Report, April 7, 2011. http://www.socialmediaexaminer.com/social-media-marketing-industry-report-2011/.
10. Taken from the Awareness e-book *The Social Marketing Funnel* 2011. http://info.awarenessnetworks.com/Social-Funnel.html.
11. Taken from the Awareness e-book *The Social Marketing Funnel* 2011. http://info.awarenessnetworks.com/Social-Funnel.html.

CHAPTER 8

1. Cohen, David, "Travel Sites Put Over 1.5 Billion Facebook Places on Map," All Facebook (allfacebook.com, Blog), November 18, 2011. http://www.allfacebook.com/facebook-travel-2011-11.
2. Charlton, Graham, "ASOS Is the Best Loved Digital Brand: Study," Econsultancy.com (blog), September 28, 2011. http://econsultancy.com/us/blog/8074-asos-is-the-best-loved-digital-brand-study.
3. Martin, Amy Jo, "To Monetize Social Media, Humanize It," Harvard Business Review, July 18, 2011. http://blogs.hbr.org/cs/2011/07/to_monetize_social_media_humanize_it.html.
4. Sorenson, Lauren, "5 Awesome Examples of Engaging Social Media Campaigns," HubSpot Blog, November 29, 2012. http://blog

.hubspot.com/blog/tabid/6307/bid/29272/5-Awesome-Examples-of
-Engaging-Social-Media-Campaigns.aspx.

5. Brogan, Chris, "How Outposts Improve Your Ecosystem,"
ChrisBrogan.com (blog), January 9, 2010. www.chrisbrogan.com/
how-outposts-improve-your-ecosystem/.

6. Green, Callan, "Killer Facebook Fan Pages: 5 Inspiring Case
Studies," Mashable, June 16, 2009. http://mashable.com/2009/06/
16/killer-facebook-fan-pages/.

7. Owyang, Jeremiah, "Matrix: Evolution of Social Media Integration
and Corporate Websites," WebStrategy Blog, March 28, 2010. http://
www.web-strategist.com/blog/2010/03/28/matrix-evolution-of
-integration-of-social-media-and-corporate-websites/.

CHAPTER 9

1. Ryan, Super Bowl Social Media Followup and Lessons Learned,"
Bacon Social Media (blog), February 29, 2012. http://www
.baconsocialmedia.com/super-bowl-social-media-command-center
-followup-and-lessons-learned/.

2. Wagner, Mitch, "Olympic Committee Gets a Medal for Social Media
Policy," TheCMOSite.com (blog), June 28, 2011. http://www
.thecmosite.com/author.asp?section_id=1137&doc_id=230828.

3. Owyang, Jeremiah, "Framework and Matrix: The Five Ways
Companies Organize for Social Business," WebStrategy (blog), April
15, 2010.

CHAPTER 10

1. Owyang, Jeremiah, "Number of Fans and Followers Is NOT a
Business Metric—What You Do with Them Is," web-strategist.com
(blog), November 17, 2011. www.web-strategist.com/blog/category/
social-media-measurement/.

2. Linnell, Nathan, "6 Key Metrics for a Social Media Measurement
Dashboard," Searchenginewatch.com (blog), December 28, 2010.
www.socialmediaexaminer.com/8-social-media-metrics-you-should
-be-measuring/.

3. Gillin, Paul, "How to Calculate Social Media ROI," gillin.com
(blog), June 24, 2010. http://gillin.com/blog/2010/06/how-to
-calculate-social-marketing-roi/.

4. Naslund, Amber, "Going Beyond Social Media Reach," Brass Tack
Thinking (blog) August 2010. www.brasstackthinking.com/2010/
08/going-beyond-social-media-reach/.

5. Awareness e-Book, *The Social Funnel*, December 2011. http://info .awarenessnetworks.com/Social-Funnel.html.

6. Awareness e-Book, *The Social Funnel*, December 2011. http://info .awarenessnetworks.com/Social-Funnel.html.

7. Suryakumar, Prashant, "Making Data Relevant: The New Metrics for Social Marketing," January 11, 2011. mashable.com/2011/01/11/ social-media-metrics/.

8. Paine, K.D., "Listening, Understanding, and Predicting the Impacts of Social Media on Your Business," May 2010 www.kdpaine.com/ tasks/sites/kdp/assets/File/SAS_Marketing_Lab_2010_05_04_ Read-Only.pdf.

9. Baer, Jay, "6 Critically Undervalued Social Media Success Metrics," Convince & Convert.com (blog), January 11, 2011. www.convince andconvert.com/social-media-roi/6-critically-undervalued-social -media-success-metrics/.

9. Solis, Brian, "Exploring and Defining Influence: A New Study," BrianSolis.com (blog), September 29, 2010. www.briansolis. com/2010/09/exploring-and-defining-influence-a-new-study/#).

10. Owyang, Jeremiah, "Framework: The Social Media ROI Pyramid," Web-Strategist.com (blog) December 13, 2010. www.web-strategist .com/blog/2010/12/13/framework-the-social-media-roi-pyramid/.

CHAPTER 11

1. eMarketer, "Social Media Presence More Important Than Social Media Ads," October 11, 2011. www.emarketer.com/Article.aspx? R=1008634.

2. Jones, Ron, "3 Tips for Improving your Online Share of Voice," ClickZ (blog), July 25, 2011. www.clickz.com/clickz/column/ 2096125/tips-improving-online-share-voice.

3. Awareness, Inc. e-Book, *The Social Funnel: Driving Business Value with Social Marketing*, Dec 2011. http://info.awarenessnetworks .com/Social-Funnel.html.

4. Van Grove, Jennifer, "Sharing on the Web: How, When, Where and Why We Do It [INFOGRAPHIC]," Mashable, October 11, 2011. http://mashable.com/2011/10/11/sharing-trends/.

Index

About the Author

Mike Lewis is the Vice President of Sales and Marketing at Awareness, Inc., a leading provider of social marketing software, headquartered in Burlington, Massachusetts. Awareness' OnDemand software drives revenue from social marketing activities for 500+ brands.

Mike is a leading expert on the impact of social marketing on business and a marketing executive with a 14-year track record of success at early-stage technology companies including StreamServe (now OpenText), Salesnet (acquired by RightNow), and RightNow Technologies (now Oracle), where he helped facilitate their growth into highly successful organizations. He has worked with several brands to help drive sales through social marketing including Sony Pictures, Major League Baseball, Starwood Hotels, Titleist, American Cancer Society, Comcast SportsNet, Zynga, Nuance, Tiger Woods Foundation, Maui Jim, and many others.

Mike is a frequent speaker at industry events and an active blogger at Socialnomics.net, SocialMediaToday.com, SocialEpisodes .com, TheCustomerCollective.com, and Business2Community.com. He served as the President of the Business Marketing Association

Boston for an unprecedented three-year term, leading the group to Chapter of the Year Award and Outstanding Programming Award in 2008. Mike earned a BA in Organizational Psychology and Business Communications from Stonehill College and an MBA from Bentley University in 2001.

Connect anytime!

Twitter: @bostonmike

Facebook: facebook.com/bostonmike

LinkedIn: linkedin.com/in/lewismich